Handwriting
A Teacher's Guide

Multisensory Approaches to
Assessing and Improving Handwriting Skills

Jane Taylor

David Fulton Publishers

London

This book is dedicated to all the children with whom I have worked, who have provided me with so much inspiration on the art of teaching handwriting.

David Fulton Publishers Ltd
Ormond House, 26–27 Boswell Street, London WC1N 3JZ

www.fultonpublishers.co.uk

First published in Great Britain by David Fulton Publishers 2001

British Library Cataloguing in Publication Data
A catalogue record for this book is available from the British Library

ISBN 1–85346–765–0

Typeset by Kate Williams, Abergavenny
Printed in Great Britain by Bell & Bain Ltd., Glasgow

Contents

Acknowledgements

My heartfelt thanks go to my husband Peter, who is a constant support and who has spent many hours checking the text and suggesting alterations.

My thanks also go to:

- my daughter, Ruth, who assisted me in deciding on a suitable format for the manual;

- Pauline Thompson, who drew the figures;

- Joyce Gurr, who painstakingly worked on the assessment sheets, checklists, records and figures;

- Liz White, Di Rankin, Janie Jarman and Sue Mountjoy of Bincombe Valley School, Weymouth, with whom I have worked closely to verify my ideas;

- Jane McNeil, Headteacher of Bincombe Valley School, who proofread the original draft; Martin Turner of the Dyslexia Institute, who provided information on assessing handwriting speed; the many colleagues in the 'handwriting world', with whom I have held numerous discussions over the years about various aspects of handwriting and its teaching;

- the proposal reviewer, Alison Kelly of the University of Surrey, Roehampton, for her constructive criticisms, which have been incorporated into the manual;

- finally, Nina Stibbe and her colleagues at David Fulton Publishers, for their invaluable support.

Introduction

Written language has been an important form of communication for many centuries. At this point in time, despite the ever-increasing use of a keyboard in the workplace, handwriting still plays a role in our society. In the home messages are still hand-written and in the early years at school the majority of pupils use pencil and paper for recording their work. Therefore the attainment of a fluent, attractive, legible hand remains a prerequisite for the majority of school children.

Handwriting is a learned, physical skill. It is a mechanical task that requires:

- the underlying cognitive and physical abilities to learn the skill,
- precise instructions in a multi-sensory and systematic manner,
- sufficient time to practise each new step,
- progress to be monitored regularly.

Adopting this approach results in handwriting that is easy to read, personally satisfying and allows the pupil to concentrate on the higher-level skills of composition.

Handwriting is closely linked with spelling. When the pupil begins to learn to spell a word each letter is traced individually. As the written trace of the letters of a word becomes automatic, a motor memory, an 'engram', is created. So learning to write letters should always be linked to meaningful letter strings and words.

Pupil's abilities vary. In the Reception class and Year 1 there will be a group of pupils who will have no difficulties in acquiring handwriting skills with the minimum of instruction and supervision, a second group who will need specific instruction and time allocated for practice to consolidate what has been taught and a third group who will need to proceed at a much slower pace. The last group will need more teaching, more practice and supervision. It is interesting to note that the first group is likely to produce more written work, the second somewhat less and the third group may remain at the pre-writing stage and not be ready for any formal handwriting instruction until Year 1 and may require further basic instruction in Year 2. As a consequence of this situation the first group has much more practice than the second and those who would benefit from plenty of practice have the least. To cater for the disparity of the three groups it will be necessary to differentiate the teaching for each group so that each can proceed at its own pace. This does not mean that the basic material presented will need to be different but that the amount of time given to grasping each step will take longer for the second group and even longer for the third. This may require the need for more practice material to be available for the second and third groups and specific teaching to be continued in Years 3 and 4. Adopting these strategies should ensure that most pupils attain an acceptable standard of handwriting.

For a few pupils whose handwriting remains slow and laborious, with an outcome so messy and dissatisfying, an alternative means of written communication such as access to a word processor may be needed. In the same way as time needs to be allotted to teaching handwriting skills, it is vital that touch-typing, computer literacy and information technology (IT) skills are taught methodically so that the full potential of the computer can be utilised.

The main purpose of this manual is to provide the busy classroom teacher with assessment procedures, record sheets and systematic strategies for teaching handwriting, but special needs coordinators, paediatric occupational therapists and physiotherapists will also find the content of this manual invaluable. Lecturers in primary education could use the material when discussing procedures for teaching handwriting with their students. Furthermore, the manual could form the basis of a training programme for language support assistants who work either on a one-to-one basis or with a small group of pupils.

The National Literacy Strategy (NLS) (Department for Education and Employment (DfEE) 1998a) states that 'literate primary pupils should have fluent and legible handwriting' and it is for this purpose that the teaching strategies of this manual are linked to handwriting requirements proposed in the NLS. They provide a continuity of approach to teaching handwriting from the Reception Year (4–5-year-olds) to Year 4 (8–9-year-olds) and provide handwriting targets that are incorporated into the framework of the Literacy Hour. However, in the crucial stages of learning to write, particularly in the early stages of beginning to learn to write, and for those children who need to proceed at a slower pace, there is insufficient time within the Literacy Hour for adequate teaching of handwriting to take place, so additional time will have to be allocated on the timetable to enable this essential skill to be mastered as quickly as possible.

The first section provides a variety of assessment tasks to ascertain whether the beginner writer has the necessary prerequisite skills for learning to write. The pupil's knowledge of letters and his ability to form letters correctly are then examined. For the older pupil methods of assessing writing speeds are indicated. Some tasks can be given to a whole class; others will need to be administered on a one-to-one basis so that the assessor can more carefully observe, record and monitor each child's performance. Checklists and record sheets are provided for this purpose.

The second section suggests teaching techniques for use with the beginner writer, commencing with matching letters, progressing to learning correct letter formation and finally learning to write on lines.

The third section covers assessment and teaching techniques for the older pupil with poor handwriting skills and therefore could be used by teachers in primary, secondary and tertiary education.

This manual concentrates on teaching handwriting to pupils without significant problems but the fourth section briefly discusses the importance of identifying underlying dysfunction(s) that may be the cause of poor handwriting. A few useful programmes and tests are highlighted.

To make this manual user friendly each teaching strategy starts with a brief introduction where the material required is listed (**A** for assessment sheets, **R** for record sheets and **E** for equipment), the purpose of the activity is described, the instructions are detailed and, finally, the evaluation and an indication of the next procedure are given. Additional notes for the teacher are written in italics.

Note: For the sake of clarity the teacher is referred throughout the manual as 'she' and the pupil as 'he'. For 'teacher' one could read another professional.

Tools of the Trade

Before embarking on any handwriting activity it is necessary to consider the 'tools of the trade', as these can affect the outcome.

Furniture

All skilled action has to be launched from a stable base. Children need a comfortable, relaxed sitting position that can only be achieved if the furniture fits the pupil, rather than the pupil adjusting his body to the furniture provided. As a rule of thumb the height of the desk should be half the pupil's height and that of the seat should be a third of his height; that is about 10–15 cm above the hollow of the knee (Brown and Henderson 1989). Adopting this practice will mean a change of attitude to classroom management and willingness to have tables and chairs of different sizes in each class-room. The alternative is to provided seat pads and foot rests for smaller pupils. It is very common for pupils to tilt the chair on to the front legs when involved with writing or on to the back legs when listening to the teacher. This is an intelligent solution to maintaining a comfortable writing posture that has to be condemned for safety reasons. The solution is to praise the pupil for the intelligent use of his body, explain the danger and offer him a wedge-shaped pad that enables the writer to maintain a more ergonomically correct posture (Mandal 1985). These can be obtained from the Children's Seating Centre (see **Resources**, p. 85).

Sloping writing surface

The use of a sloping surface, such as the Write Angle (Philip & Tacey) or the Posture Pack (Children's Seating Centre), brings the work more in line with the eyes and reduces strain on the neck. Alternatively, a large A4 file can be used, placed in the landscape position. Pupils who experience pain when writing may find it helpful to work on a sloping surface.

Wooden/plastic letters

Wooden or plastic three-dimensional (3D) letters with ligatures are essential equipment. They provide sensory, visual and tactile information about letters, enabling the pupil to learn about the orientation of letters, their similarities and differences and their relationship to one another. Wooden letters are more suitable for the younger pupil whereas plastic letters are more appropriate for the older pupil.

Pencil, pens and fountain pens

There are a huge variety of pencils and pens of varying quality on the market. When selecting any writing implement it is important to consider the shape and comfort of the shaft as well as the writing point. The width of the shaft may vary and can assist in reducing the amount of tension used to grip the instrument. Pencils and pens with triangular shafts are available and may help pupils to grip the shaft correctly (see **Pencil/pen hold**, p. 49). The quality of pencil and nature of the lead will affect the outcome. The lead is graded according to its hardness and softness. H2 is very hard; H, hard; HB, average; B, soft; and B2, very soft. A soft pencil produces a more pronounced mark compared to a hard pencil. All pencils should be a reasonable length and reasonably sharp.

In the case of felt-, fibre-, plastic-tipped and roller-ball pens it is necessary to select one with a tough, long-lasting tip. The amount of contact that the tip of the pen has with the paper and the ink flow are other factors to consider.

With fountain pens the width and quality of the nib need to be taken into account. The width of the nib can make a dramatic change to the appearance of a pupil's handwriting. Many stationers will allow customers to test a pen but it is helpful to have a sample of pens that older pupils can try.

The changeover age from a pencil to pen is an ongoing debate. Until research can better inform us, the changeover is an arbitrary decision which each school must make.

Tool grips

These are a variety of grips which can be added to a pencil to provide a reminder, and can therefore be an aid to obtaining a tripod grip, but they are not a panacea. Tri-Go and Grippies (both available from LDA Living and Learning) are particularly good. More recently, new pens have a softer, spongy grip area.

Lined paper

Lined paper should be used from the beginning so the pupil can learn to appreciate how each letter relates to the lines (see Figure 1). Notice that each line is different. The slightly thicker line indicates the base line. All letters relate to the base line. Some

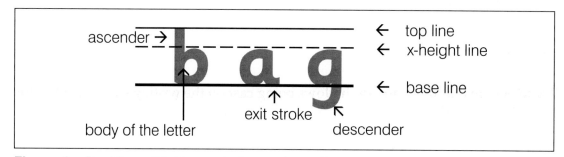

Figure 1   Position of letters relative to base line

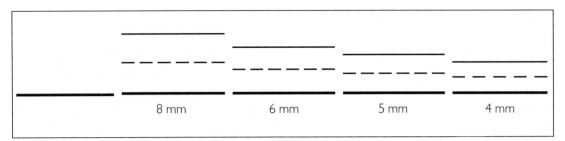

Figure 2   Recommended line spacings

letters sit on the base line; others, such as **g,** are written through the base line. The dotted line indicates the starting position of x-height letters, and the faint top line the starting position of letters with ascenders (see **Learning to Write Lower and Upper Case Letters and Numerals – Task 3**, p. 57). Learning to write using lines of this type should help the pupil to establish the correct starting position of letters from the beginning and to keep the relative size of letters constant. Pupils will require narrower line spacing as their handwriting develops (see Figure 2). Once a pupil's handwriting is automatic, first the top line and then the x-height line can be dispensed with, so finally the pupil is only using a base line. A teacher is free to use other types of lined paper. Many older pupils with handwriting difficulties may find lined paper with the base and x-height line indicated helpful.

Three sheets of paper, **E1**, **E2** and **E3**, are provided (pp. 5–7). Sheet **E1** is for the younger pupil who is beginning to describe what he has drawn and has two lines at the bottom for writing. **E2** is three-lined paper, as described above, and **E3** is conventional single-lined paper. These sheets can be used to create a standard when assessing.

There are two additional sheets of paper to be used as line guides: **E4** has a solid black line to indicate the x-height size of letters; and **E5** has sloping lines, which a pupil can use to assist them to maintain a regular slope. Both these guidelines will be easier to see it they are photocopied on to yellow card. The appropriate card can then be placed under conventional lined paper.

A4 white board

Small white boards are now available commercially. These can be useful for demonstration purposes and for the pupil's first attempt at improving letter formation. Lines can be marked on the board with a permanent ink pen.

Lighting

Try to ensure that there are no shadows being cast on the writing surface, either by sunlight or electric light, as these can be distracting.

Classroom organisation

Pupils should be facing the white board whenever handwriting is being demonstrated. Ideally, the table on which the pupils are writing should be clear of clutter so that the writing arm is always supported on the table.

Left-handers should always sit on the left of right-handers (see Figure 3) so that the writing arms of both the left- and right-handers are not restricted. All pupils should be made responsible for remembering this important fact.

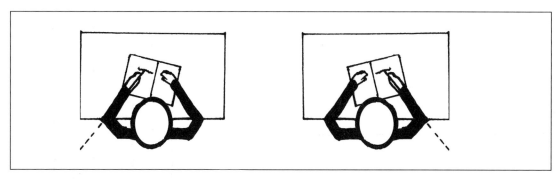

Figure 3   Correct seating arrangement and paper position for the left- and right-hander

Cursive script

Before the advent of the National Curriculum (DES 1989) pupils used print script (ball and stick) where letters do not have ligatures (exit strokes) and words are written in an unjoined manner. Since its introduction, pupils have been expected to learn a cursive script (see Figure 4). There are different schools of thought as to what constitutes a cursive script. For some all letters are joined; for others letters with descenders are not joined; and for yet others all letters, as well as all being joined, begin with an entry stroke from the base line.

What is most important is that letters that end on the base line **a b c d e h i k l m n p s t u x z** are taught with exit strokes from the beginning. This facilitates an easy transition from learning to write a single letter to learning to join it to the next letter, when diagonal and horizontal joins and joins to oval have been taught. Once a pupil can form a letter correctly and automatically, and knows how to join letters correctly, he is ready to learn to use a joined script. A few pupils may never acquire sufficient skills to master a fully joined script.

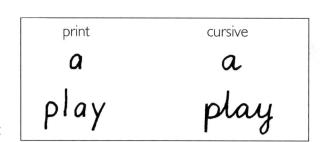

Figure 4   Types of script

4

a b c d e f g h i j k l m n o p q r s t u v w x y z

Name ....

Date ....

E2

Name ....

Date ....

Name.. Date ....

E3

E4

E5

Assessment and Records

Shape Copying

Copying shapes is a prerequisite to learning to write letters. Letters are made up of lines and circles, in a variety of orientations and curves, so it is important to know whether a pupil is able to copy the basic shapes. Berry (1997) states that a child should be able to copy a circle at 3 years, a cross at 4 years 1 month, a square at 4 years 6 months and a triangle at 5 years 3 months. The ability to copy these shapes with ease would suggest that the pupil is ready to master handwriting skills.

If he is unable to copy these shapes he is likely to encounter problems with basic letter formation and should continue with pre-writing activities for a while. If he is able to copy the first three shapes but is unable to copy a triangle then letters with diagonal lines and diagonal joins may well prove difficult to execute. Similarly, if he is unable to copy the figure of eight on its side and the flowing **o** above and below the line, he may find joining letters problematic.

There are several reasons why a pupil may experience difficulty in copying shapes. It may simply be that he lacks experience and/or sufficient maturity. However, it may also be that he has an underlying motor and/or perceptual dysfunction that would require further investigation and subsequent intervention (see **Identifying Underlying Causes of Poor Handwriting**, p. 81).

Equipment
Shape Copying **(A1)** and a ruler.

Purpose
To provide the teacher with a means of assessing whether the pupil's shape-copying ability is age appropriate and whether he can write his name using correct letter formation and placing them on the base line correctly.

> **Instructions**
> 1. Present the pupil with **Shape Copying (A1)**.
> 2. Ask him to copy each shape in the space provided.
> 3. Ask him to write his name on the dotted line.
>
> *In order to observe an example of the older pupil's fine motor skill the dotted line could be erased. Ask him to use a ruler to draw a line in the space and to write his name on the line.*

Evaluation
This task establishes whether the pupil:

- needs to spend more time on pre-writing activities (see p. 46);
- is ready to start learning to write;
- needs further practice in writing letters of his name.

Shape Copying

Date ....

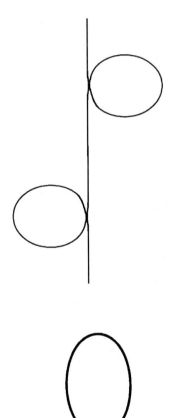

A1

Draw a Person – Draw a Clock

Some pupils with handwriting problems appear to have difficulty in transferring 3D 'real-life' images into an age-appropriate 2D form. Although there may be no direct correlation between a pupil's ability to draw and handwriting outcome, it is useful to set handwriting ability within the context of other pen and paper tasks. Some of the younger pupils may not be ready to draw a clock.

Equipment
Draw a Person – Draw a Clock (A2)

Purpose
To provide the teacher with the opportunity to observe the pupil's level of performance in these two tasks.

Instructions
1. Present the pupil with **Draw a Person – Draw a Clock (A2)**.
2. Ask him to draw a person (not a stick person) in the box on the left.
3. Ask him to draw a clock face, to include all the numerals and the two hands indicating a time, in the box on the right.

Evaluation
This task establishes a pupil's ability in relation to his peers. The teacher should note any obvious discrepancies, as this may be an indication of underlying difficulties.

Draw a Person – Draw a Clock

Name ....

Date ....

Letter Matching – Lower and Upper Case Letters

To write a letter the pupil needs to have some means of identifying it. He can do this by visual matching or by knowing its name and/or sound. Being able to match letters is a vital first step in 'knowing' a letter.

Equipment
Make two copies of the **Matching Lower Case Letters (A3)** and **Matching Upper Case Letter (A4)** sheets. Cut up one copy of each sheet so that there is a set of lower case and a set of upper case letters.

Purpose
To establish the letters which the pupil is able to match.

Instructions
1. Present the pupil with the **Matching Lower Case Letters (A3)** and the set of lower case letters in random order.
2. Ask him to match each letter.
3. Repeat this task using **Matching Upper Case Letters (A4)**.

Evaluation
This task establishes the extent to which the pupil has mastered this skill. Once the pupil can match a letter satisfactorily he can begin to work through the tasks in **Learning About Letters – Task 2** (p. 53).

Matching Lower Case Letters

a	b	c	d	e	f	g
h	i	j	k	l	m	n
o	p	q	r	s	t	u
v	w	x	y	z		

Matching Upper Case Letters

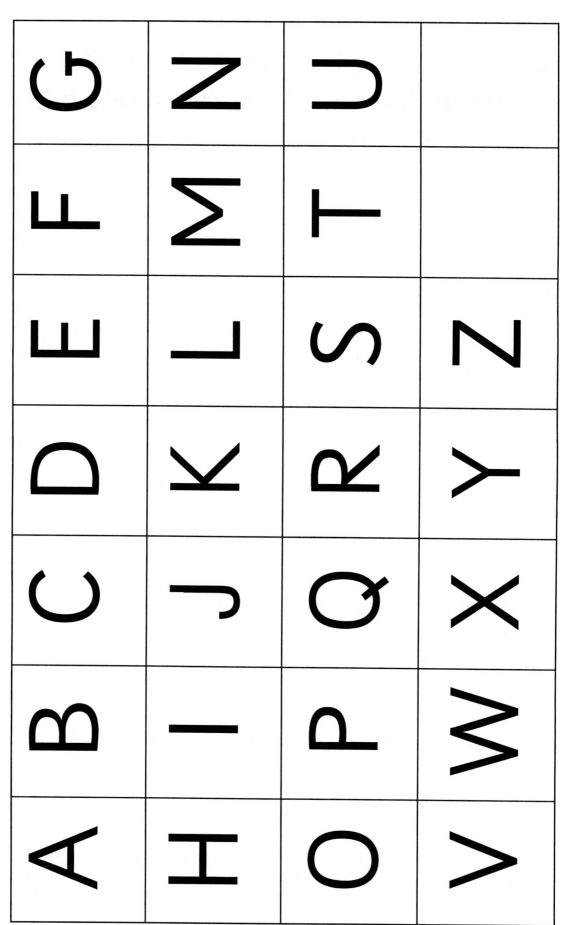

A	B	C	D	E	F	G
H	I	J	K	L	M	N
O	P	Q	R	S	T	U
V	W	X	Y	Z		

Identification of the Sound and Name of Lower Case Letters, Numerals and Upper Case Letters

A focus of the NLS Framework for pupils in the Reception Year is to learn the sound and name of lower and upper case letters (DfEE 1998). Knowledge of the sounds and names of letters is a basic skill that will assist in the mastery of handwriting, reading and spelling. In handwriting activities pupils should be encouraged to refer to letters by name as soon as possible.

Identification and the writing of numerals is not mentioned in the NLS but is included in this assessment because writing numerals correctly should be considered part of a handwriting programme (see **Learning to Write Lower and Upper Case Letters and Numerals – Task 7**, p. 60).

Equipment
- **Lower Case Letters, Numerals and Upper Case Letters (A5).**
- **Letter and Numeral Knowledge and Formation: Individual Checklist (R1)** (p. 30) on which to record pupil's responses as they are made.
- **Class Record: Letter Knowledge, Sound and Name (R2 and R3)** (pp. 32, 33).

Purpose
To establish whether the pupil knows the sound and name of the lower and upper case letters and the names of the numerals.

Instructions
1. Present the pupil with the **Lower Case Letters, Numerals and Upper Case Letters (A5).**
2. Point to each letter and ask him to state the sound of each lower case letter.
3. Point to each letter and ask him to state the name of each lower case letter.
4. Point to each letter and ask him to state the sound of each upper case letter.
5. Point to each letter and ask him to state the name of each upper case letter.
6. Point to each numeral and ask him to state the name of each numeral.
7. Enter the results on the **Letter and Numeral Knowledge and Formation: Individual Checklist (R1).**
8. If appropriate, enter the results on the **Class Record: Letter Knowledge, Sound and Name (R2).**

Evaluation
This task establishes which letters require further teaching or practice. Once he can identify a letter by its name and/or sound and has sufficient pencil skills he can begin to work through the tasks in **Learning to Write Lower and Upper Case Letters and Numerals – Task 2** (p. 57).

Note

The lower case letters on **A5** are grouped in 'families' according to their formation. This enables the teacher, when assessing letter forms, to see at a glance whether the pupil is experiencing difficulty with the correct letter formation with letters of one particular family or with a number of unrelated letters. For the sake of consistency the same order is used for upper case letters.

Lower Case Letters, Numerals and Upper Case Letters

c	a	d	g	o	s	e	f	i	t
l	u	y	j	r	n	m	p	h	b
k	v	w	x	z	q				

0	1	2	3	4	5	6	7	8	9	10

C	A	D	G	O	S	E	F	I	T
L	U	Y	J	R	N	M	P	H	B
K	V	W	X	Z	Q				

© Jane Taylor, *Handwriting: A Teacher's Guide*, David Fulton Publishers, 2001

A5

Lower Case Letter and Numeral Formation (copying) and Upper Case Letter Formation (copying)

The NLS Framework for the Reception Year requires pupils to learn to write lower case letters using the 'correct sequence of writing movements' for each letter (DfEE 1998). Capital letters are also introduced at this stage with further consolidation to take place in Year 1.

In the early stages of mastering handwriting skills, the pupil may not be able to write a letter from memory but may be able to copy it using correct letter formation. The teacher will need to watch each pupil individually as he completes this task in order to ascertain which letters and numerals are being formed correctly and, in the case of incorrect letter forms, noting where the error is occurring.

Equipment
- **Lower Case Letter and Numeral Formation (copying) (A6)**.
- **Letter and Numeral Knowledge and Formation: Individual Checklist (R1)** (p. 30).
- **Upper Case Letter Formation (copying) (A7)**.
- **Class Record: Lower Case Letter and Numeral Formation (R4)** (p. 34).
- **Class Record: Upper Case Letter Formation (R5)** (p. 35).

Purpose
To establish which letters and numerals the pupil is able to copy correctly.

Instructions
1. Present the pupil with the **Lower Case Letter and Numeral Formation (copying) (A4)**.
2. Ask him to copy each letter, pointing to the guideline where the first letter is to be copied. *Do not indicate where the remaining letters are to be copied or comment on the guideline provided.*
3. Watch him as he performs this task and note any errors in letter formation.
4. Enter the pupil's results on the **Letter and Numeral Knowledge and Formation: Individual Checklist (R1)** and, if appropriate, on the **Class Record: Lower Case Letter and Numeral Formation (R4)** and **Class Record: Upper Case Letter Formation (R5)**.
5. Repeat these tasks using **Upper Case Letter Formation (copying) (A7)**.

Evaluation

This task establishes those letters that the pupil can copy correctly, those that require further practice and those that he still needs to learn. If he is able to copy letters correctly he can proceed to **Learning to Write Lower and Upper Case Letters and Numerals – Task 3** (p. 57).

Filling in the information for an individual pupil on the Class Record (**R4** and **R5**) will enable the teacher to monitor the individual's performance in relation to his peers and to plan appropriate work for different groups within the class. This task can be used at regular intervals to monitor progress.

Note

The lower case letters on **A6** are grouped in 'families' according to their formation. This enables the teacher, when assessing letterforms, to see at a glance whether the pupil is experiencing difficulty with the correct letter formation with letters of one particular family or with a number of unrelated letters. For the sake of consistency the same order is used for upper case letters.

Lower Case Letter and Numeral Formation (copying)

Name .... Date ....

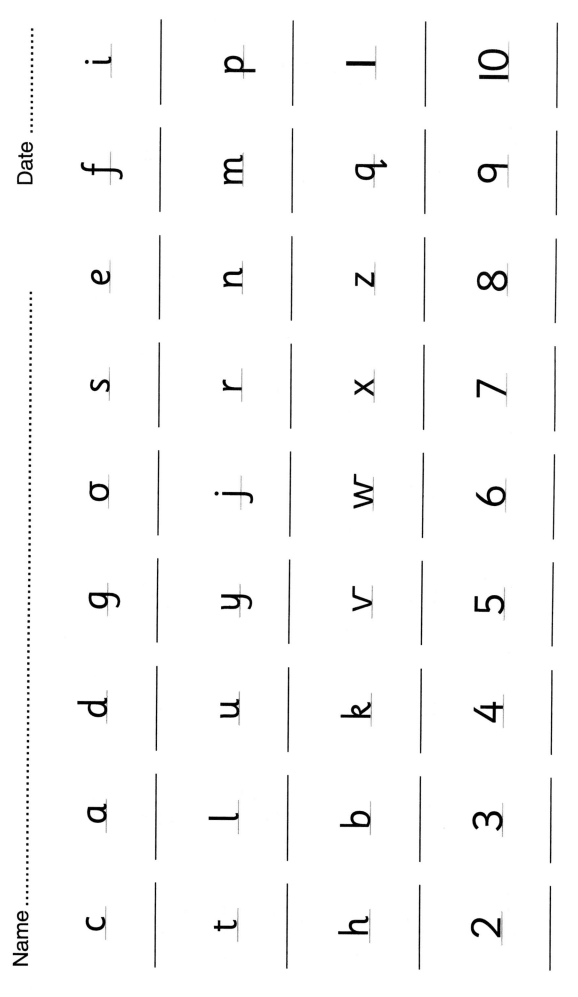

c	a	d	g	σ	s	e	f	i
t	l	u	y	j	r	n	m	p
h	b	k	v	w	x	z	q	l
2	3	4	5	6	7	8	9	10

Upper Case Letter Formation (copying)

Name ....

Date ....

C	A	D	G	O	S	E	F	L
T	L	U	Y	J	R	N	M	P
H	B	K	V	W	X	Z	Q	

Lower and Upper Case Letter and Numeral Formation (dictation)

To be an efficient writer the pupil needs to be able to write letters from memory using correct letter formation in response to a given name or sound.

Equipment
- **Lower Case Letters, Numerals and Upper Case Letters (A5)** (p. 21) to use for dictation.
- **Lower and Upper Case Letter and Numeral Formation (dictation) (A8).**
- **Letter and Numeral Knowledge and Formation: Individual Checklist (R1)** (p. 30).
- **Class Record: Lower Case Letter and Numeral Formation (R4)** (p. 34).
- **Class Record: Upper Case Letter Formation (R5)** (p. 35).

The teacher can decide whether she is going to refer to letters by their name or sound when administering this test. A mixture of both name and sounds should not be used.

Purpose
To enable the teacher to establish whether each letter (both lower and upper case) and numeral is correctly or incorrectly formed. In addition she can ascertain whether the pupil is able to write the lower case letters of the alphabet from memory.

Instructions

Task 1
1. Present the pupil with the **Lower and Upper Case Letter and Numeral Formation (dictation) (A8)** sheet.
2. Tell him that you are going to dictate each letter and that you want him to write one lower case letter in each box. Emphasise that upper case letters are not to be used. *Do not comment on the guideline provided.*
3. Dictate one lower case letter.
4. Watch as he performs this task and note any errors in letter formation. *If the pupil writes a letter that was not dictated the teacher may repeat the letter.*
5. Repeat these tasks, asking him to write upper case letters.

Task 2
1. Ask the pupil to write the numerals 0–1 in the remaining boxes.

Task 3
1. Ask the pupil to write out the lower case letters of the alphabet in alphabetical order on the first line below the boxes. This exercise can be timed and the

A8

result entered on the sheet. *Stipulate whether the letters are to be written in an unjoined or cursive script, i.e. letters joined, according to the school policy.*

2. Ask the pupil to write the upper case letters in alphabetical order on the second line.

Enter the pupil's results on the **Letter and Numeral Knowledge and Formation: Individual Checklist (R1)** and, if appropriate, on the **Class Record: Lower Case Letter and Numeral Formation (R4)** and **Class Record: Upper Case Letter Formation (R5).**

Evaluation

These tasks establish which letters require further teaching and practice and the extent of the pupil's ability to write out the letters of the alphabet in order. If the pupil needs to work on letter formation proceed to **Learning to Write Lower and Upper Case Letters and Numerals – Task 3** (p. 57). If the pupil can form all letters with ease and fluency proceed to **Joins** (p. 67).

Filling in the information for an individual pupil on the Class Record **R4** and **R5** will enable the teacher to monitor the individual's performance in relation to his peers and enable her to plan appropriate work for different groups within the class.

These tasks can be used at regular intervals to monitor progress.

Letter and Numeral Formation (dictation)

Name ....

Date ....

¦	¦	¦	¦	¦
¦	¦	¦	¦	¦
¦	¦	¦	¦	¦
¦	¦	¦	¦	¦
¦	¦	¦	¦	¦
¦	¦	¦	¦	¦
¦	¦	¦	¦	¦
¦	¦	¦	¦	¦

Letter and Numeral Knowledge and Formation: Individual Checklist

In order to plan appropriate instruction and to monitor progress, it is important to record, at regular intervals, the extent of each pupil's alphabet and numeral knowledge and his ability to form letters and numerals correctly.

Equipment
- Letter and Numeral Knowledge and Formation: Individual Checklist (R1)

Purpose
To record each pupil's lower and upper case letter and numeral knowledge and his ability to form letters and numerals correctly. In addition to record which hand the pupil uses for writing and whether his tool hold is satisfactory or poor and whether he needs to use a tool grip.

Instructions
1. Insert the pupil's name, class and the date in the appropriate spaces on the right of the **Letter and Numeral Knowledge and Formation: Individual Checklist (R1).**
2. Place a tick in each box if he:
   - is able to match, name and sound the letter;
   - can copy the letter using correct letter formation;
   - can write the letter from dictation using correct letter formation.
3. Place a tick in each box if he:
   - knows the name of each numeral;
   - matches each numeral;
   - forms each numeral correctly.
4. Note which hand he uses, whether his tool hold is satisfactory or poor and whether he needs to use an additional grip.

Evaluation
From the information collated the teacher can see at a glance which letters require further teaching and/or practice.

Letter and Numeral Knowledge and Formation: Individual Checklist

Name ....

Class ....

Date ....

- [ ] left-handed
- [ ] right-handed
- [ ] tool hold satisfactory
- [ ] tool hold poor

needs to use tool grip

	yes	no

	c	C	a	A	d	D	g	G	o	O	s	S	e	E	f	F	i	I
match																		
name																		
sound																		
copied																		
dictated																		

	t	T	l	L	u	U	y	Y	j	J	r	R	n	N	m	M	p	P
match																		
name																		
sound																		
copied																		
dictated																		

	h	H	b	B	k	K	v	V	w	W	x	X	z	Z	q	Q
match																
name																
sound																
copied																
dictated																

	0	1	2	3	4	5	6	7	8	9	10
match, name												
formation												

Class Record: Letter Knowledge, Sound and Name

R2

R3

R4

R5

Details in the class records enable the teacher to know each pupil's performance in relation to his peers, to monitor progress and to plan future handwriting sessions.

Equipment
- **Letter and Numeral Knowledge and Formation: Individual Checklist (R1)** (p. 30)
- **Class Record: Lower Case Letter Knowledge, Sound and Name (R2)**
- **Class Record: Upper Case Letter Knowledge, Sound and Name (R3)**
- **Class Record: Lower Case Letter and Numeral Formation (R4)**
- **Class Record: Upper Case Letter Formation (R5)**

For **R2** and **R3**, a dotted line divides each box. The left-hand space is to record whether the pupil knows the sound of the letter. The right-hand space is to record whether he knows the name of the letter. The teacher might find it easier to use two different coloured pens, one to indicate the letters that were copied and the other to indicate the letters that were written from dictation.

Purpose
To collate information from **Letter and Numeral Knowledge and Formation: Individual Checklist (R1)** on to **Class Records (R2–R5)**.

Instructions
1. Insert the pupil's name in the appropriate column.
2. Tick each correct response and dot each incorrect response.

Evaluation
This task enables the teacher to identify, at any one time, each pupil's knowledge of letters and numerals and his ability to form them. It helps her to see at a glance whether there are any letters that are still causing difficulties to a number of pupils. In addition, it serves to highlight left-handers and those with poor grip. A + sign may be used to indicate the need to use an additional grip.

Class Record: Lower Case Letter Knowledge, Sound and Name

Name	c	a	d	g	o	s	e	f	i	t	l	u	y	j	r	n	m	p	h	b	k	v	w	x	z	q

Class ....

Date ....

© Jane Taylor, *Handwriting: A Teacher's Guide*, David Fulton Publishers, 2001

Class Record: Upper Case Letter Knowledge, Sound and Name

Name	C	A	D	G	O	S	E	F	I	T	L	U	Y	J	R	N	M	P	H	B	K	V	W	X	Z	Q

Class ....

Date ....

Class Record: Lower Case Letter and Numeral Formation

Name	c	a	d	g	o	s	e	f	i	t	l	u	y	j	r	n	m	p	h	b	k	v	w	x	z	q	l	1	2	3	4	5	6	7	8	9	10	lh	g

dictated ☐   copied ☐

Class ....   Date ....

© Jane Taylor, *Handwriting: A Teacher's Guide*, David Fulton Publishers, 2001

Class Record: Upper Case Letter Formation

Name	C	A	D	G	O	S	E	F	I	T	L	U	Y	J	R	N	M	P	H	B	K	V	W	X	Z	Q

dictated ☐   copied ☐

Class ....   Date ....

Legibility and Speed

Handwriting is a secretarial skill where speed – that is the ability to produce letters quickly with ease and fluency – and legibility – that is the 'ability to recognise a letter, number, or word easily and correctly outside of the context of the word, sentence, or phrase' (Hasbrouck *et al.* 1994) – are critical. Legibility requires the adequate execution of letter formation, encompassing letter size, slant, alignment and spacing. Although there are many complex factors affecting an individual's performance at any specific time, measuring handwriting production enables the teacher to assess whether a pupil can maintain legibility when writing at speed and / or the speed is adequate for the demands of the curriculum. In this test the pupil is engaged in a copying task, a more mechanical task compared with free written expression that requires more thought.

There is a choice of three sheets. Sheet **A9** is suitable for the younger pupil, **A10** for the pupil whose handwriting is becoming speedier or the pupil with reading and spelling difficulties, and **A11** for the older pupil. These sheets only use a base line but alternative line spacing could be used.

Equipment
Select appropriate **Legibility and Speed (A9–A11)** sheet.

The task should be presented in the same manner each time. Any change, for example from using a pencil to using a pen, should be noted, as this may affect the outcome.

Purpose
To enable the teacher to monitor both the legibility and the speed of a pupil's handwriting.

Instructions

When testing an individual, the first two sections can be timed and a note made of the writing speed in the space provided. The phrase and sentence in the third section should be written as continuous text.

Sheets A9–A11

For the first and second sentence:
1. Present the pupil with the appropriate **Legibility and Speed** sheet.
2. Ask him to read the first line and then to copy it in his 'best' writing.
3. Ask him to read the second line and to copy it in 'ordinary' writing, i.e. that which he uses when writing his news or story.

If a pupil struggles to read any of the text, note this at the bottom of the sheet.

Sheets A9 and A10
For the third section:
1. Ask the pupil to read the third line.
2. Ask him to write the phrase as many times as possible in two minutes.

Sheet A11
For the third sentence:
1. Ask the pupil to read the third line, ensuring that he has added the 's' rather than an 'ed' ending to jump.
2. Ask him to write the sentence as many times as possible in three minutes.
3. The teacher or pupil counts the number of letters written and divides the total by the number of minutes. The resulting figure represents the number of letters written per minute.
4. The teacher and pupil look at the handwriting and note particular letters and joins that are incorrectly or poorly formed. These can be entered on the appropriate record sheet.

Evaluation
This task establishes the pupil's handwriting speed. If his handwriting is slow then the teacher can consider whether this is due to an underlying dysfunction (see **Identifying Underlying Causes of Poor Handwriting**, p. 81) that should be investigated or whether he needs more practice in writing at speed (see **Writing Letters Speedily and Automatically**, p. 62).

Table 1 presents a summary of writing speeds conducted by a number of researchers using the phrase 'cats and dogs' or the sentence 'The quick brown fox jumps over the lazy dog'. Note that Ziviani used the phrase 'cats and dogs' in her initial research (1984) and 'cat and dog' in the recent study (1998). These norms should only be used as a general indicator of attainment unless precise conditions of the original research are replicated. Alternatively, data can be collected from all pupils within a class to create class norms. Another possibility is to compare an individual's performance from one time to the next.

Table 1 Summary of copying speeds (compiled from Alston 1992 and Ziviani and Watson-Will 1998)

	Ziviani 1984	New Zealand 1980	Pickard and Alston 1985	Pickard and Alston 1985	Wallen et al. 1996	Ziviani and Watson-Will 1998	Ziviani and Watson-Will 1998
Educational grade	3–7	Year 1 Intermediate	Year 1 Secondary	Year 1 Secondary	Grade 3–12	Grade 3–7	Grade 3–7
Age range		11–12 years	11–12 years	11–12 years		7–12 years	7–12 years
Participants	575	3738	149	149	1292	189 boys	183 girls
Instructions	A	B	C	C	D	A	A
Text	cats and dogs	The quick brown fox jumps over the lazy dog.	The quick brown fox jumps over the lazy dog.	I love cats and dogs.	The quick brown fox jumps over the lazy dog.	cat and dog	cat and dog
Method	Copy for 2 minutes	Copy for 3 minutes	Copy for 3 minutes	Copy for 3 minutes	Copy for 3 minutes	Copy for 2 minutes	Copy for 2 minutes
Speed	Letters per minute	Letters per minute	Letters per minute	Letters per minute	Letters per minute	Letters per minute	Letters per minute
Age						mean	mean
7	33				54	34.90	38.77
8	34				57	45.79	55.95
9	38				64	67.00	70.45
10	46				81	73.06	83.30
11	52	77	82	97	94	89.50	83.07
12		77	82	97	100	110.76	84.68
13					115		
14					116		
15					124		
16					133		

A. Write as quickly as possible. Do not correct. Write as many times as possible. (Pencil on lined paper.)
B. Write as many times as possible.
C. Write as quickly as possible in writing which can be read.
D. Write as quickly but as neatly as you can. (On lined paper.)

Legibility and Speed

Name .... Class .... Date ....

The quick brown fox jumps over the lazy dog.

The big dog sat on the red rug.

cat and dog

A9

Legibility and Speed

A10 Name .... Date ....

The quick brown fox jumps over the lazy dog.

_____

_____

[ ]

The big dog sat on the red rug.

_____

_____

[ ]

cat and dog

_____

_____

_____

_____

_____

Class .... [ ]

Legibility and Speed

Name ....   Date **A11**

The quick brown fox jumps over the lazy dog.

_____

_____

The quick brown fox jumps over the lazy dog.

_____

_____

The quick brown fox jumps over the lazy dog.

_____

_____

_____

_____

_____

_____

_____

_____

_____

_____

Class ....

Assessment of Written Language Ability: Timed Tests

Although this manual is concerned with the mechanics of handwriting, handwriting performance speed may be affected when the older pupil is engaged in free written expression. He may be able to copy at an acceptable speed but when recording his thoughts on paper his written output is noticeably slower than that of his peers. A variety of methods to obtain such a measure are suggested. These tests are more suitable for pupils over 8 years old. Two different sheets of lined paper are supplied (**E2**, p. 6 and **E3**, p. 7): **E2** is for the pupil who is able to express himself on paper but is using three-lined paper; **E3** is for the older pupil who writes on conventional paper with a base line.

Equipment
Select the appropriate sheet of lined paper.

Purpose
To establish whether a pupil's apparent slowness in writing is due to difficulty in expressing his thoughts on paper.

Instructions

Word test
1. Ask the pupil to write all the words he can recall. *The teacher can decide on an appropriate time limit. The same time limit should be used on subsequent occasions.*

Ten-minute test (Thomson and Watkins 1990)
1. Select ten words of appropriate spelling age and write them on the top of the A4 sheet of paper provided.
2. Present the sheet to the pupil.
3. Ask him to write a sentence for each word. The time allowed is ten minutes.
It may be necessary to have an additional sheet of ten words for the fast workers.

Sentence test (Hedderly 1995)
This test consists of 40 sentences. Each begins with a phrase. A time limit can be set and the number of words calculated. Norms and standard deviations are provided for 9-year-olds through to adult, with separate norms for 17- and 18-year-olds who are in, or not in, full-time education.

20-minute test (Alston 1992)
1. Present the pupil with the sheet of the A4 paper.
2. Ask the pupil to write on one of the following subjects:
   * My favourite person/personality
   * Someone I know very well
   * My life history
   * Something in which I am very interested.
   The time allowed is 20 minutes.

On completion of the task ask the pupil to count the number of words that he has written. The total is divided by the number of minutes that have been allowed. The result represents the number of words per minute.

Many dyslexic pupils find it difficult to sustain writing for 20 minutes. If the teacher is working with an individual she may choose to shorten this exercise to five minutes, which is sufficient time for composition and spelling difficulties to begin to become obvious.

Evaluation

The teacher may wish to refer to the summary of research on writing speed in Table 2 in order to consider a pupil's performance relative to norms. These norms should only be used as a general indicator of attainment unless the precise conditions of the research are replicated. Correspondence with the Dyslexia Institute suggests that, on average, 13-year-olds are writing 14–15 words per minute and 15-year-olds write closer to 16–18 words per minute. Alternatively, data can be collected from all pupils within a class to create class norms. Another possibility is to compare an individual's performance from one time to the next.

Table 2 Summary of free writing speed (Alston 1992)

Alston 1990
Age range, 8–11 years; Participants, 168; Duration, 20 minutes
Topic: My favourite person/personality

Age	Average words per minute	Range of words per minute
8	3.75	1–11
9	5.65	1–15
10	6.00	2–16
11	7.65	3–20

Dutton 1989
Age range, 13–17 years; Participants, 100; Duration, 30 minutes
Topic: My life history

Age	Average words per minute
13	12.50
14	14.00
15	16.00
16	17.00
17	18.50

If the pupil has written significantly fewer words than his peers, the teacher should note the characteristics of his written work. For example, syllable, word and sentence length, and type of spelling errors made. His poor written output may be symptomatic of underlying difficulties that should be investigated at the earliest opportunity. Meanwhile programmes can be created to encourage him to improve his writing skills. *Assessing and Promoting Writing Skills* (Alston 1995) could be used for this purpose.

Pupils with dyslexia frequently have difficulty expressing themselves with written language so an appropriate diagnostic test should be administered to establish whether this is the case.

The pupil can be asked to complete the **Self Evaluation Checklist (R7)** (p. 77) by closely examining his handwriting in this task.

Early Teaching Strategies

Pre-writing Activities

Pupils arrive in school with a variety of skills. A number of them will have had plenty of experience in using writing tools and may be able to write some letters, but may not form them correctly. Others may be at the pre-writing stage and will need to spend a considerable amount of time on pre-writing activities before embarking on the formal stages of learning to write letters.

It is important that pupils master the necessary fine motor and perceptual skills before being exposed to the world of letters and are expected to write in a formal manner. This section is not intended to be comprehensive but describes a few ways of developing pre-writing skills and learning about letters. *Curriculum Guidance for the Foundation Stage* (Qualifications and Curriculum Authority (QCA) 2000) is a detailed document, full of ideas 'intended to help practioners plan to meet the diverse needs of all children'. It stresses the importance of being competent in a number of key skills and highlights the 'stepping stones' that 'show the knowledge, skills, understanding and attitudes that children need to learn during the foundation stage in order to achieve the early learning goals'. The section on physical development is particularly relevant to the pre-writing pupil, with the section on communication, language and literacy providing useful ideas for the pupil who is beginning to make marks on paper.

Painting

Most children enjoy painting. Painting at an easel encourages gross motor movement, particularly around the shoulder girdle, which in turn will make for greater postural stability when writing.

Colouring

Cursive writing demands a complicated series of movements as the pupil writes words horizontally across a sheet of paper. It involves both the up/down strokes executed by the fingers, the circular movement of the thumb and the side-to-side movements executed by the wrist. Learning to colour and to control the colouring tool within the framework of an outline is one way in which these fine motor movements may be practised. Whenever the pupil is using a crayon or felt-tip pen, he should be encouraged to hold it between the pads of the thumb and index finger and resting on the middle finger; an efficient tool grip (see Figure 8, p. 49). Whenever the pupil is using a writing instrument he should be encouraged to hold it in the manner already described.

Drawing

Drawing 'offers even the least mature child a ready means of creativity and expression' (Michael, undated). The teacher should show interest in what the pupil has drawn by wanting to 'read' the drawing. She can encourage him to use more detail in his drawings so that there is more to 'read'. This will give him opportunities to make plenty of fine motor movements with his pencil or crayon. Thomas (1997) suggests that a face cut from a magazine can be pasted on to a sheet of paper and then the pupil draws in the clothes and inserts patterns on them.

It takes time to include detail in drawing so a picture may take more than one session. As the pupil's proficiency increases, the idea of drawing a sequence of pictures to make a story can be introduced. Sheet E1 (p. 5), provided for this purpose, is a photocopiable sheet of paper in landscape orientation, divided into three with a line at the bottom on which the 'story' could be written.

Patterns

Tracing over and copying patterns is another useful activity (see Figure 5). It is important that the **o** is an oval and not a circle. Patterns can be done at an easel with paint, or on a flat surface. When drawn on a large piece of paper gross motor movement will be involved. When executed with a variety of tools, or traced with the index finger in sand or flour, fine motor movements will be used. The same patterns can be repeated or they can be intertwined with one another. The pattern can be repeated across the width of the paper, which is a pleasurable experience. An alternative, as a precursor to writing words, is to repeat the pattern as illustrated, followed by a space. Continue repeating the pattern in this manner across the page.

Figure 5   Writing patterns

During this stage the pupil can begin to become familiar with letters by handling 3D wooden or plastic letters (see **Learning About Letters**, p. 53).

Language of instruction

Many words used by teachers when referring to letters are about space and order: for example, bottom, middle, top, before, after, next to. The pupil may not be familiar with these concepts so time should be spent ensuring that these words are understood in the pre-writing phase.

The Four Ps

A pupil should learn that handwriting is a physical skill that demands attention to detail. Learning how to sit, to use a 'presser', the optimum position in which to place the paper and how to hold the writing tool are all important and can be remembered as the '4Ps': posture, presser, paper position and pencil/pen hold.

Posture

The teacher should establish, from the beginning, the importance of adopting a good writing posture that prevents unnecessary muscle strain and future chronic backache. The thighs should be placed well back in the chair with the feet flat on the floor (see Figure 6). There should be sufficient room for the forearms to rest on the table. The elbows should be fairly close to the body to give support to the shoulder girdle. The non-writing hand should support the work, which in turn allows the forearm to support the body and to enables the writing arm to move freely. The distance from the eyes to the paper should be approximately the distance between the knuckles and elbow.

Figure 6   Correct sitting position

Presser

Most adults do not choose to write on a single sheet of paper on a hard surface yet pupils are frequently expected to draw, colour or write on a single piece of paper placed directly on the table. All pupils should be provided with a piece of stiff card or some other form of presser on which to place their work. The left-hander might benefit from having a thin strip of card pasted on to the presser to indicate the paper position (see Figure 7).

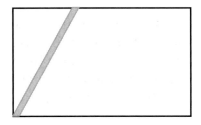

Figure 7   Suggested form of presser

Paper position

The angle of the paper is crucial for the left-hander (see Figure 3, p. 4).

1. The left-hander needs to be able to see what he is writing. This can be achieved if the paper is angled sufficiently towards the left with the writing hand below the base line.
2. The forearm should be parallel with the edge of the paper.
3. The non-writing hand should be placed on the paper *above* the writing hand. This ensures that the writing hand is not restricted and is free to move across the paper. This should prevent a hook grip from developing.

The angle of the paper is not crucial for the right-hander. A more natural posture is achieved when the bottom corners are angled to the right. The non-writing hand should be used to support the paper to prevent it moving.

All pupils need to learn that the optimum position for writing is in the middle of a sheet of paper, so they will need to be reminded to push the paper up at regular intervals and not move the forearm down. The majority of worksheets are written on A4 paper in the portrait mode. Worksheets presented in the landscape mode would be more appropriate for the younger pupil.

Pencil/pen hold

Between the ages of 3½ and 6, a pupil's grasp should develop from a static tripod grip, where there will be more than one finger on the barrel, to the dynamic tripod grip, where the tool is held between the pads of the thumb and index finger (see Figure 8). This method of grasping the writing tool is certainly efficient and therefore one that pupils should be encouraged to use.

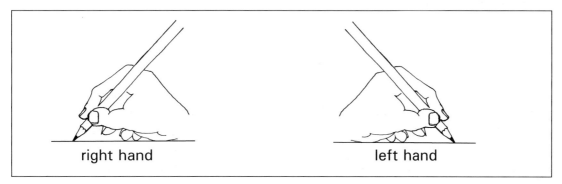

right hand   left hand

Figure 8   Correct tool hold

A number of pupils tend to hold the pencil very near the point. This restricts fine motor movements and makes it more difficult for the pupil to see what they are writing. The left-hander should be encouraged to hold the pencil at least 2 cm from the point. As a guide, pupils should be told to hold the pencil on the coloured part of the shaft and not on the wood at the tip. An elastic band can be put on the barrel to indicate the finger and thumb position.

A tense grip may cause pain and increase the amount of pressure that the pupil exerts when writing. Pressure is obvious because the trace of the writing can be seen on the reverse side of the paper. A 2B pencil that produces a darker trace or a pencil with a lead that breaks easily can be tried.

Pain may also be due to poor gross and/or fine motor control and these difficulties should be addressed with a special physical education programme or by referral to a paediatric occupational therapist or physiotherapist.

It is difficult for many pupils over the age of 8 to change a poor grip. If the writing is slow and very laborious then it may be worth encouraging a pupil to try to change his grip in which case the use of a Tri-Go or the Stubby grip might be helpful. For the pupil who has developed a very tense grip, which might also cause pain, there is an alternative grip. The writing tool is placed between the index and middle finger, with the tool resting on the middle finger and the index finger resting on the barrel. The barrel is held between the pad of the thumb and the middle finger.

The 4P routine

It is vital that the 4P routine is established as the pupil's responsibility from the beginning. This should be considered an essential element in the mastery of handwriting skills. A poster illustrating the 4Ps (posture, presser, paper position and pencil hold) could act as an *aide-mémoire*.

Suggested Order for Teaching Letters and Numerals

There is no correct or incorrect order for teaching letters. However, the pupil's learning load is lessened if letters are taught in 'families' where there is a similarity in the movement pattern to produce them. He can begin to learn to notice the parts of letters that are similar and those that are different (see Figure 9).

Remember that all letters that end close to the base line **a b c d e h i k l m n p s t u x z** must be taught with exit strokes.

Figure 9 Typical letter family

Lower case letters

Note: The black letters in each group are written with similar movement patterns whereas the grey letters only use some of the movement patterns.

- Straight line letters **i t l**.
- Oval letters: **c a d g** e s f (to avoid confusion **q** can be taught later when diagraphs are introduced as it always is followed by **u**).
- Humpy letters: **r n m p h b k**.
- Cup shaped letters: **u y** j.
- Zigzag letters: **v w** x z.
- **o** is an oval letter but should be taught separately as it starts in the 12 o'clock position.

The trouble with **e**

Many pupils find **e** a difficult letter to form correctly. The problem is knowing where to start **e** and then how to form it correctly. One solution is to start the letter **e** on the base line using a diagonal line that is drawn nearly to the x-height line and then is taken over the top in an anticlockwise direction and is continued in the same manner as the letter **c**. This will make the diagonal join from letters **a c d e h i k l m n t u**

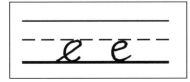

Figure 10 The two forms of the letter **e**

to **e** very easy. On the other hand if **e** is to join to **o r v w** then the **e** should be started in the centre of the x-height (see Figure 10). Both types of **e** will need to be taught. In addition the teacher needs to consider the implications of these facts if the pupil has the letter **e** in his name and decide which form of **e** will be taught first.

Capital letters

The movement patterns of capital letters are based on straight lines and curves so most children find them easier to write. Capital letters can also be taught in 'families'. Remember, capital letters start at the top and are the same size as letters with ascenders. *Note:* **I** and **J** are written without serifs. When a pupil is using a cursive script so that the difference between an upper case **I** and a lower case **i** is obvious, the use of serifs is unnecessary.

- Oval letters which start at 1 o'clock: **C G S**.
- Oval letters which start at 12 o'clock: **O Q**.
- Straight line letters: **E F H I L T**.
- Zigzag letters: **A V W M N X K Y Z**.
- Humpy letters: **B D P R**.
- Cup letters: **U J**.

Numerals

Many pupils do not write numerals correctly. Numerals are frequently reversed and/or started at the bottom. Numerals can also be taught in 'families'. Remember, numerals start at the top and are the same size as capital letters or letters with ascenders.

- The initial movement for **1** and **4** is straight down; **5** can also be started in this manner.
- The initial movement for **2** and **3** is clockwise. This is also applicable to the second movement of **5**. The second movement of **3** is a repetition of the first movement. The scond movement of **2** is a diagonal line. The third movement for **2** and **5** is a left-to-right horizontal straight line.
- The initial movement for **6** is a downward movement and then round in an anti-clockwise direction.
- The initial movement for **7** is also a left-to-right straight horizontal line.
- **8** can be started with the same movement pattern as **S** and finish with a diagonal line.
- **9** can be started with a **c** written above the x-height line but completed with a straight line which ends on the base line.
- The **1** and **0** in the numeral **10** should be the same height.

Learning About Letters

The young pupil should have plenty of experience handling 3D letters before he is expected to work with letters in two dimensions so sets of wooden/plastic alphabet letters with ligatures can be used to learn to match letters. The three tasks that follow are for pupils at the pre-writing stage.

Task 1: Learning to match lower and upper case letters

In the early stages of learning to write a pupil may not be able to recall letter names and/or sounds. However, if he is required to write a letter he should have a mental picture of the shape of that letter. Learning to match letters is one way that this can be achieved and is a first step in learning to identify letters.

Equipment

Two copies of the **Matching Lower Case Letters (A3)** (p. 17) and **Matching Upper Case Letters (A4)** (p. 18) sheets. Cut up one copy of each sheet so that there is a set of lower case and a set of upper case letters.

Purpose

To learn to match lower and upper case letters.

> **Instructions**
> 1. Present the pupil with the **Matching Lower Case Letters (A3)** sheets and the set of lower case letters in random order.
> 2. Ask him to match each letter.
>
> Repeat these tasks using the **Matching Upper Case Letters (A4)**. This task can be repeated by matching lower case letters to upper case letters and vice versa.

Evaluation

This task establishes which letters the pupil recognises and which letters need further practice. Once he can match a letter satisfactorily he is ready learn the name and/or sound of letters and proceed to **Tasks 2** and **3**. Rolling modelling clay into sausages and making it into letter shapes is a useful activity for this stage.

Task 2: Learning more about letters

The more aware the pupil is about the characteristics of letters, the easier it will be for him to master writing letters on lines correctly. This task develops the pupil's spatial awareness of letters and an appreciation of the relative height of letters and their orientation with the base line.

Equipment

A set of wooden/plastic letters with ligatures. Photocopy sheet **E6** (p. 55) on to two sheets of card.

Purpose

To help the pupil to learn to identify x-height letters, letters with ascenders and descenders, letters with dots, oval and straight line letters, and to begin to appreciate how each letter relates to the base line.

Instructions

1. Present the pupil with all the letters of the alphabet and the two sheets of **E6** on card.
2. Ask him to identify all the letters which are x-height.
3. Ask him to place them on the line correctly.
4. Check that the task has been completed correctly.

This task can be repeated to discover which letters are oval, have ascenders, descenders, straight lines or dots.

Evaluation

Once the pupil is aware of how each letter relates to the base line proceed to **Task 3**.

Task 3: Matching lower case letters to a given name/sound

The NLS requires pupils in the Reception Year to be able to give the sound and name for each lower and upper case letter of the alphabet (DfEE 1998).

Equipment

Two copies of the **Matching Lower Case Letters (A3)** (p. 17) and **Matching Upper Case Letters (A4)** (p. 18) sheets. Cut up one copy of each sheet so that there is a set of lower case and a set of upper case letters.

Purpose

To learn the name and the sound of the letters.

Instructions

1. Present the pupil with the **Matching Lower Case Letters (A3)** and a set of lower case letters in random order.
2. State a letter name and ask him to select the letter with that name.
3. Ask him to indicate where that letter is on the sheet and to place his chosen letter on the sheet.
4. Repeat the tasks with the remaining letters of the alphabet.
5. Repeat these tasks stating the sound of each letter.

Repeat these tasks using the **Matching Upper Case Letters (A4)**.

Evaluation

This task establishes which letter names and sounds the pupil knows and which ones need further practice. Once he knows a letter's name or sound proceed to the tasks in **Learning to Write Lower and Upper Case Letters and Numerals** (p. 56).

Learning to Write Lower and Upper Case Letters and Numerals

The NLS Framework expects pupils in the Reception Year to learn to write their first name and to begin to be able to write each lower case letter using the correct movement patterns (DfEE 1998). As he will frequently be asked to write his name on his work, the logical letters to start with are the letters in his name.

The tasks presented below provide a step-by-step method of helping the pupil to achieve this goal. Once he has mastered writing his name, he can then proceed to learn to write the remaining letters of the alphabet using the same techniques.

Pupils will be at different stages of letter knowledge so the teacher will have to decide whether she is going to refer to letters by name or sound. Do not use a mixture of names and sounds.

Task 1: Matching and naming the letters of the pupil's name

Equipment
A set of wooden or plastic letters. Make a name card by drawing silhouettes of the letters of his name on a piece of card using the 3D letters.

Purpose
This task teaches the pupil to identify the letters in his name by matching them first with the pre-selected letters of his name and then from a random selection of letters.

Instructions
1. Place the name card on the table and then put down the 3D letters of his name one by one, simultaneously saying the name of each letter.
2. Ask the pupil to match the letters on to the silhouettes, reminding him to name the letters as he matches them on his card. *The order does not matter for the first attempt. On the second attempt and thereafter the left-to-right order should be stressed.*
3. Repeat this task until the pupil can place the letters on the name card with ease. *Several sessions may be required for the pupil to become efficient at this task.*
4. Ask the pupil to turn the name card face down and to place the letters of his name in the correct order on the table.
5. Ask him to check the letters of his name for accuracy by referring to his name card.

Evaluation
Once the pupil is able to recall the order of letters in his name with ease he is ready to move on to **Task 2**.

Task 2: Tracing letters of the pupil's name

The next stage is for the pupil to learn to write each letter of his name.

Equipment
The pupil's name card. No writing implement is used in this task.

Purpose
To teach the pupil to begin to learn the correct letter formation of the letters of his name by tracing the silhouettes of the letters of his name with his index finger.

Instructions
1. Select a letter from the pupil's name that will be the simplest to write. Letters with straight lines are the easiest.
2. Name the chosen letter and indicate the starting position of the letter.
3. Mark the starting position with a green dot.
4. Ask him to put his index finger of his writing hand on the dot. Hold his hand and help him trace the correct movement pattern. Ask him to say the name of the letter as he writes it.
5. Ask him to trace the letter by himself. Remind him to say the letter. *Repeat this stage until he is using the correct movement pattern.*
6. Ask him to extend his writing arm to shoulder height and point straight ahead with his index finger.
7. Ask him to form the shape of the letter. *The teacher can refer to this activity as 'Writing letters in the air'.*
8. Ask him to close his eyes and then to write a given letter in the air.

Repeat these instructions with the remaining letters of his name, beginning with letters that are in the same 'family'; i.e. those that have similar movement patterns. Remember to spend time indicating the similarities of letters in the same 'family'.

Evaluation
Once the pupil is able to trace the letters of his name correctly and is beginning to identify each letter by name he is ready to move on to **Task 3**.

Task 3: Appreciating the relative height of letters

Equipment
A set of 3D wooden/plastic alphabet letters with ligatures and sheet E6, photocopied on to two pieces of A4 card.

Purpose
This task is to teach the pupil that:
*   Letters vary in height in three ways:
    - **b d f h k l** are letters with ascenders (tall letters); **t** is not quite so tall;
    - **f g j p q y** are letters with descenders (letters with tails).
    - **a c e i m n o r s u v w x z** are x-height letters (body letters or middle size letters).

- Letters **b d h k g p q y** have an x-height component as well as ascenders or descenders.
- All letters relate to the base line.
- Letters **a b c d e h i k l m n o r s t u v w x z** all sit on the base line.
- Letters **f g j p q y** are written through the base line.

Instructions
1. Place the cards in front of the pupil.
2. Show him how each plastic/wooden letter of his name relates to the base line.
3. Ask him to place the plastic/wooden letters of his name in the correct position on the line.

Evaluation
Once the pupil is able to relate the letters of his name to the base line proceed to **Task 4**.

Task 4: Writing letters in sand/flour/shaving foam

Equipment
Cover a tray with a layer of sand or flour. Alternatively spray shaving foam over an area of the table. These media are used because it enables the pupil to feel the movement pattern as he writes and to see a clear trace of the letter just written.

Purpose
This task can be used to help the pupil begin to learn to write the letters of his name using his index finger to write the letters.

Instructions
1. Place the sand tray in front of the pupil in the portrait position.
2. Demonstrate how to draw the base line from left to right, about two-thirds of the height of the tray from the top of the tray, using your index finger.
3. Shake the tray to smooth the sand.
4. Ask the pupil to draw the line using his index finger.
5. Starting with the simplest letter, demonstrate how to write it stressing its relationship to the base line. If it ends on the base line emphasise the exit stroke that can be verbalised as a 'kick' or 'flick'.
6. Ask him to write the letter.
7. Ask him to close his eyes and then to write the letter in the air.
8. Repeat these instructions with the remaining letters of his name.

Once he can form the letters of his name correctly the remaining letters of the alphabet can be learnt using the same instructions.

Evaluation
Once the pupil has mastered writing his name correctly he can proceed to **Task 5**.

Task 5: Writing letters on the hand

An additional way to practise letter formation is for the pupil to write letters on his hand (Ramsden 1992). This is an excellent exercise because he can watch and feel the movement pattern of a letter. It is particularly useful for the left-hander because the exit strokes are traced along the thumb.

Purpose
To reinforce the pupil's acquisition of correct letter formation.

Instructions
1. Ask the pupil to hold out his non-writing hand with the palm facing upwards.
2. Explain to him that the whole of the palm represents the body of the letter, the fingers the ascenders and the forearm the descenders.
3. Ask him to write a letter on his hand.

Evaluation
Once the pupil has gained a greater appreciation of the relative height of letters proceed to **Task 6**.

Task 6: Writing lower and upper case letters using lined paper

Before embarking on any writing task it is important to remind the pupil of the Four Ps routine (p. 50) so that the pupil begins to take responsibility for his posture, paper position and tool hold. If he is left-handed he needs to check that he is sitting in the correct place (see Figure 3, p. 4) in relation to the pupil next to him.

Equipment
Photocopy sheet **E2** (p. 6) or use another type of lined paper where there is a line to represent the x-height.

Purpose
To enable the pupil to become competent at writing on three-lined paper.

Instructions
1. Ask the pupil to write out a given lower case letter three times.
2. Ask him to tick the well-formed letters.
3. Ask him to write the given letter as many times as possible in a stated time. Remind him that only the well-formed letters are ticked. *The teacher chooses an appropriate time according to the pupil's ability.*
4. Ask him to tick the well-formed letters.
5. Ask him to count the number of letters that he has written and the number of ticks and to make a note of these.

*The cross stroke for **t** and **f** should be on the x-height line.*
Repeat these instructions for upper case letters.

Evaluation

This task establishes the letter forms that the pupil is able to write fluently and automatically, and shows whether the pupil is developing a self-critical approach to the appearance of his handwriting. He is ready to proceed to **Writing Letters Speedily and Automatically** (p. 62) and **Joins** (p. 67).

Task 7: Numeral formation

Numerals are frequently reversed or formed from the bottom. Before embarking on writing numerals, insure that the pupil is able to orientate 3D numerals correctly. **Tasks 4** and **5** can be adapted for use with numerals.

Equipment
A set of wooden or plastic numerals 1–10 and a photocopy of sheet **E2** (p. 6)

Purpose
To enable the pupil to write the numerals using the correct formation.

Instructions
1. Ask the pupil to write the numerals **1–10** and ask him to notice where he starts each numeral.
2. Select one of the poorly formed numeral and demonstrate how it should be formed using arrows to indicate the correct movement pattern.
3. If a numeral is written from the base line give him the rule 'All numbers start at the top'.
4. Ask the pupil to write out the numeral once. If it is correctly formed ask him to write it out three times.
5. Ask him to decide on the well-formed numerals and give each one a tick.
6. Ask the pupil to shut his eyes to write the numeral in the air or to write out the numeral again. *A successful attempt indicates that the pupil has begun to internalise the form of the numeral.*
7. Give the pupil a selection of pairs of numerals containing the numeral just practised. Tick the well-formed numerals.

If 2 3 7 are reversed
1. Ask the pupil to draw an arrow across the top of the board or his book to indicate the direction in which words on a page are read.
2. Select one numeral and demonstrate how, when the first movement is made in the direction of the arrow, the numeral will be correctly written.
3. Follow teaching procedures 4–7 above.

If 4 5 6 are reversed
1. Ask the pupil to draw an arrow across the top of the board or his book to indicate the direction in which words on a page are read.
2. For **4** demonstrate how the first movement is down and across and then a small line down is added. For **5** demonstrate how the first movement is down. The next

movement is round in the direction of the arrow. The last movement is to return to the top of the numeral and draw a straight line in the direction of the arrow. For **6** demonstrate how the first movement is down. The next movement is round in the direction of the arrow.

3. Follow teaching procedures 4–7 above.

If 8 *is incorrectly written*

1. Ask the pupil to start the **8** as a capital **S** and then draw a straight line back to where the letter began.
2. Follow teaching procedures 4–7 above.

If 9 *is incorrectly written*

1. Ask the pupil to start to write a lower case **a** above the x-height line and, instead of the exit stroke, to give it a straight line descender.
2. Follow teaching procedures 4–7 above.

Evaluation

Numerals should now be formed correctly.

Writing Letters Speedily and Automatically

The essence of successful handwriting is being able to produce accurately formed letters automatically and speedily. Berninger and Graham (1998) suggests that once a pupil is able to write correctly formed letters automatically he is in a position to concentrate on the higher level writing skills. This assessment can be used in the early stages of learning to write letters correctly and subsequently when the pupil is learning to join letters.

Two Alphabet Speed sheets are provided: **Alphabet Speed (A12)** is for pupils who are using three-lined paper; **Alphabet Speed (A13)** is for older pupils who are using a single base line.

As the teacher will need to monitor the accuracy of letter formation, this test should be administered individually or with a small group. It can be repeated at frequent intervals until the pupil can write all the letters of the alphabet correctly in one minute.

Equipment
Select the appropriate Alphabet Speed sheet.

Purpose
To write all the letters of the alphabet as speedily as possible while maintaining correct letter formation.

Instructions
1. Present the pupil with the Alphabet Speed sheet.
2. Ask him to insert the date in the first of the two boxes.
3. Ask him to place his pencil on the base line.
4. Tell him that he is to write out the alphabet as fast as he can when you say 'Go'. Tell him that he must put his pencil down when you say 'Stop'. Remind him that the letters must be well formed.
5. Set the stop-watch for one minute.
6. On completion of the task ask him to tick the well-formed letters.
7. Ask him to count the number of ticks and record the results in the second box.

In order to establish whether any inaccuracies in letter formation or joins occur when vision is excluded, this task can be repeated with eyes shut or covered. Inaccuracies are due to incomplete mastery of the ability to write automatically.

Evaluation
This exercise should enhance the pupil's ability to write both lower and upper case letters automatically and speedily. It enables the pupil to become self-critical by evaluating whether he is forming letters and joins correctly. In addition, the teacher is able to monitor each pupil's progress in relation to his peers.

Alphabet Speed

Name .... Class **A12**

Alphabet Speed

A13 Name .... Class...........................

_____

_____ ☐

_____

_____ ☐

_____

_____ ☐

_____

_____ ☐

_____

_____ ☐

_____

_____ ☐

_____

_____ ☐

_____

_____ ☐

_____

_____ ☐

_____

_____ ☐

_____

_____ ☐

_____

_____ ☐

_____

_____ ☐

_____

_____ ☐

_____

_____ ☐

Once pupils have mastered correct letter formation and handwriting is becoming automatic, handwriting teaching and practice should become intrinsically bound up with spelling, following the targets in the NLS Framework. In addition, handwritng should also be seen as part of any teaching situation across the curriculum whenever an opportunity presents itself. For instance, the subject may be 'Butterflies', say, but before the teacher writes the word on the board, she might ask the pupils to list the details that have to be remembered about the letter **f**. She could then ask a pupil to write the letter on the board. Errors in handwriting should be part of any assessment of written work and corrections should be undertaken immediately and then checked (see **Corrections**, p. 71).

Punctuation

The NLS Framework requires pupils in Year 1, Term 1, to begin to use a capital letter at the start of a sentence and to end it with a full stop (DfEE 1998). By the end of Year 1 they should be using capital letters for names and the personal pronoun I, and know how to use a question mark. The comma is introduced in Year 2, Term 2, and speech marks in Year 3, Term 1. Appreciating their function requires syntactical and linguistic understanding. However, the pupil needs to be taught how to write and position punctuation marks correctly.

The full stop

A full stop should be placed on the base line immediately after the last letter of a sentence.

Purpose
To learn to position the full stop correctly.

> **Instructions**
> 1. Demonstrate the position of the full stop.
> 2. Dictate a short sentence to the pupil.
> 3. Tick the full stop if it is correctly placed.

Evaluation
The pupil is able to position the full stop correctly in his written work.

The question mark

A question mark should be placed on the base line immediately after the last letter of a sentence and should be the same height as an upper case letter. Follow instructions 1–3 above.

The comma

A comma should be placed on the base line immediately after the last letter of a phrase with the descending tail hanging below the line. Follow instructions 1–3 above.

Speech marks

How speech marks are written and their position will need to be taught. Follow instructions 1–3 above.

Joins

The NLS Framework requires pupils to begin using and practising diagonal and horizontal joins to letters with and without ascenders at the beginning of Year 2 (DfEE 1998). The word that a pupil will write most frequently is his name, so learning to join the letters in his name is a useful place to start. In order for pupils to consider handwriting to be an essential component of writing, and not a once a week activity called handwriting practice, emphasis on learning how to join letters should be intrinsically linked to the requirements of the word level and sentence level work as set out in the NLS Framework. It may be necessary to set aside time outside the Literacy Hour to introduce the various joins.

The alphabet line

The alphabet line (see sheet **E7**, p. 70) shows letters with the joins indicated by a dotted line. In two lines the letters with descenders do not have joins: in the other two lines the letters all have joins. Numerals 1–10 are at the end of the alphabet line. This sheet can be photocopied and cut into strips and placed on the table as a useful *aide-mémoire*.

Horizontal joins

Horizontal joins are the easiest to master. They are from letters **o r v w**, which end on the x-height line. Horizontal joins to letters that start on the x-height line should be introduced first, followed by horizontal joins to letters with ascenders. There are a number of details that will need careful teaching. The length of the horizontal line from the **o** has to be increased to accommodate half the width of the **o** when it is joined to letters starting on the x-height line (see Figure 11). Horizontal joins to oval

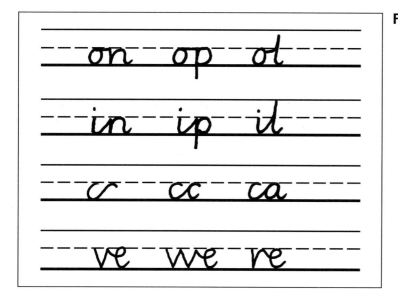

Figure 11   Joins

letters must be demonstrated and learned, as these also require the length of the join to be extended in order to accommodate the letter.

Purpose
To master horizontal joins.

Instructions
1. Ask the pupil to write out the alphabet and decide which letters end on the x-height line.
2. Ask him to identify all letters that end on the x-height line.
3. Choose a letter string (e.g. **on**) and demonstrate the horizontal join.
4. Ask him to write out a given letter string three times.
5. Ask him to tick the well-formed joins.
6. Ask him to write the given letter string as many times as possible in a stated time. Remind him that only the well-formed joins are ticked. *The teacher chooses an appropriate time according to the pupil's ability.*
7. Ask him to tick the well-formed joins.
8. Ask him to count the number of joins that he has written and the number of ticks and to make a note of these.

Follow instructions 3–8 for practising horizontal joins to letters with ascenders.

Evaluation
The pupil should gradually be using horizontal joins in all written work.

Horizontal joins to *e*

The letter *e* in high frequency words, such as **love**, **we** and **are**, require the letter *e* to be formed in a different manner and the horizontal join from **v w r** will need to be modified (see Figure 11).

Purpose
To master joining the horizontal letters to **e**.

Instructions
1. Ask the pupil to write the letter **w** followed by the letter **e**. Explain that the modified **e** will need to be used.
2. Demonstrate how the join from **w** has to be dropped a little to accommodate the starting position of **e**.
3. Follow instructions 4–8 above.

Follow the above instructions for letters **v** and **r**.

Evaluation
The pupil should gradually be using a horizontal join to **e** in all written work.

Diagonal joins

To create a fluent style diagonal joins should be at an angle of approximately 45°. A useful verbal clue is to tell the pupil that the diagonal join is like writing one half of the letter **x**. The teacher should ensure that the pupil is able to execute diagonal lines at 45° before introducing joins to letters. It should first be remembered that pupils who cannot draw a triangle might find this join difficult to execute accurately (see **Shape Copying**, p. 12). Letters **a c d e h i k l m n u x z**, which end on the base line, join to the subsequent letter with a diagonal join. Diagonal joins to x-height letters should be introduced first and then introduce diagonal joins to letters with ascenders (see Figure 11).

Purpose
To master diagonal joins.

> **Instructions**
> 1. Ask the pupil to write out the alphabet and decide which letters end on the base line.
> 2. Choose a letter string (e.g. **in**).
> 3. Follow instructions 4–8 (p. 68).
>
> Demonstrate the diagonal join to letters with ascenders in the same manner.

Evaluation
The pupil should gradually be using diagonal joins in all written work.

Diagonal joins to oval letters

The diagonal join to oval letters **a c d g s** is not mentioned in the NLS Framework. This is a very common join that many pupils fail to learn to execute correctly (see Figure 11).

Purpose
To master the diagonal join to oval letters.

> **Instructions**
> 1. Ask the pupil to write out the alphabet and decide which are the oval letters.
> 2. Choose the letters **c** and **a** and demonstrate how the diagonal join to **a** has to curve over at the x-height line in an anticlockwise direction to accommodate the letter **c**. A useful verbal tag is 'Make a hook to hang the letter on'.
> 3. Demonstrate how the letter **a** fits neatly into the curve. A useful verbal tag is 'Go back round the roundabout'.
> 4. Follow instructions 4–8 (p. 68).

Evaluation
The pupil should gradually be using diagonal joins in all written work.

It is relatively easy for a pupil to learn how to join letters in a handwriting lesson but putting the newly acquired skill into practice takes time and encouragement.

Alphabet Line

abcdefghijklmnopqrstuvwxyz 1234567890

abcdefghijklmnopqrstuvwxyz 1234567890

abcdefghijklmnopqrstuvwxyz 1234567890

abcdefghijklmnopqrstuvwxyz 1234567890

Corrections

To ensure that the pupil considers handwriting to be an integral part of written expression, handwriting faults should be considered part of the assessment of a piece of written work. Faults should be indicated and corrections should be executed immediately after the appraisal takes place. If the work is in an exercise book then the back pages can be used for these corrections. If the pupil is using a worksheet then the reverse side or the bottom of the sheet can be used.

Purpose
To make handwriting corrections an integral part of a lesson.

Instructions
1. Draw the pupil's attention to the poorly formed letter.
2. Ask the pupil whether he knows how to write the letter or demonstrate how the letter should be written.
3. Ask him to write out the letter once.
4. If he writes it correctly, ask him to write out the letter three times.
5. Tick all the well-formed letters.
6. Set the stop-watch and ask him to write out the letter repeatedly. *Choose an appropriate length of time.*
7. Tick all the well-formed letters.

The pupil should find this form of practice more worthwhile and make more of an effort to try to incorporate that which has been practised into future written work. It is very important for the teacher to commend the pupil when this happens.

Teaching Strategies for Pupils with Poor Handwriting

Teaching Strategies for the Poor Handwriter

This section of the manual is concerned with the pupil whose poor secretarial skills are affecting his ability to perform at the level required by the curriculum. Incorrect letter formation and joins in the early stages of learning to write, often leads to illegible handwriting as the demands of the curriculum increase. Early recognition of a problem enables remedial action to be taken in good time.

The teacher needs to decide whether the pupil's difficulties are because he has missed a crucial stage in learning basic handwriting skills or are caused by an underlying dysfunction. The underlying dysfunction will need to be addressed (see **Identifying Underlying Causes of Poor Handwriting**, p. 81). Whatever intervention is decided on, the pupil will probably need to be taught the mechanics of handwriting as outlined in this manual. The point of breakdown in the pupil's handwriting can be established by using the assessments:

- **Shape Copying (A1)** (p. 13)
- **Draw a Person – Draw a Clock (A2)** (p. 15)
- **Lower Case Letters, Numerals and Upper Case Letters (A5)** (p. 21)
- **Letter and Numeral Formation (A8)** (p. 28)
- **Legibility and Speed (A9–A11)** (p. 39–41)
- **Assessment of Written Language Ability: Timed Tests** (p. 42)
- **Alphabet Speed (A12, A13)** (pp. 63, 64).

Once the assessment is complete there are number of ways forward. The teacher can decide exactly what the pupil needs to learn. This is an appropriate route to choose if the pupil is below the age of 9. Alternatively, she can ask the pupil whether he has already been told what is wrong with his handwriting or whether he is aware of any faults that he would like to correct and then work from there. A third approach, which an older pupil may find novel, is to ask him to complete the **Self Evaluation Checklist (R7)** (p. 77) and then for him to decide on learning objectives with the help of the teacher, if necessary. In order to keep a record of present performance the teacher may wish to fill in the **Individual Handwriting Record (R6)**.

Individual Handwriting Record

The **Individual Handwriting Record (R6)** enables the teacher to record present performance. In order to ensure that all details are noted, the record should be filled in as soon as the assessment has taken place by examining the handwriting on the various assessment sheets just completed. These samples of handwriting should be kept as they provide a benchmark by which the teacher and pupil are able to monitor change and progress. A pupil can be very encouraged when he looks back over previous work and observes the improvement he has made. The **Individual Handwriting Record (R6)** can also be used at regular intervals to record progress.

Individual Handwriting Record

Administered by .... Date ....

Name .... Date of Birth .... Age ....

School .... Class

Handedness   Right ☐   Left ☐   Unresolved ☐

Prerequisite Skills

The pupil holds his pencil with a tripod grip?	YES / NO
The pupil sits comfortably facing the desk?	YES / NO
The paper is positioned correctly?	YES / NO
The non-writing hand is placed on the paper?	YES / NO
The pressure is appropriate?	YES / NO
There is no evidence of tremor?	YES / NO

Letter and Numeral Formation

	c	a	d	g	o	s	e	f	i	t	l	u	y	j	r	n	m	p	h	b	k	v	w	x	z	q
Knows letter sound																										
Knows letter name																										
Letter formed correctly																										
Letter reversed/inverted																										

Numerals from 1 - 10 formed incorrectly ....

Written Language Ability

Legibility and Speed Test

The quick brown fox jumps over the lazy dog.   **The big dog sat on the red rug.**

best writing   lpm ☐   best writing   lpm ☐

ordinary   lpm ☐   **cat and dog**

written at speed lpm ☐   written at speed lpm ☐

Free written expression wpm ☐

Legibility

Letters are the correct size	YES / NO
Letters are straight and parallel	YES / NO
Spacing between letters is regular	YES / NO
Spacing between words is regular	YES / NO
Letters align to the base line correctly	YES / NO
The use of capitals letters is appropriate	YES / NO
The use of full stops is appropriate	YES / NO

Learning Objectives 1. ....

2. ....

Self Evaluation Checklist

The **Self Evaluation Checklist (R7)** is a useful tool to use with older pupils who have frequently been told to improve their handwriting with little direction as to how this might be achieved. The use of the checklist **(R7)** changes the emphasis from the teacher telling the pupil what to correct to the pupil discovering his own strengths and weaknesses. He may be surprised to discover that there are only one or two areas of difficulty that need further practice and therefore be more enthusiastic about working on improving his handwriting. Furthermore the teacher is in a position to praise him for all the positive aspects of his handwriting in the evaluation.

Equipment
Self Evaluation Checklist (R7) and samples of the pupil's handwriting which will be on the completed assessment sheets **Letter and Numeral Formation (A8)** (p. 28), **Legibility and Speed (A9–A11)** (pp. 39–41) and **Assessment of Written Language Ability** (p. 42).

Purpose
To enable the pupil to establish those things which he does well and those that require further work.

Instructions
1. Present the pupil with the checklist and his samples.
2. Ask him to read one statement at a time and to decide how it applies to him or to his writing. *The pupil may be unable to evaluate his performance due to lack of knowledge so he may need demonstrations or further explanations before being able to complete a section of the checklist.*
3. Ask him to put a tick in the appropriate box.
4. Ask him to notice in which column the majority of his ticks fall. *He may be quite surprised to find the majority of ticks are in the All, Yes or Most boxes with only a few in the Some, None or No boxes.*
5. Praise him for all the positive aspects of his handwriting.
6. Ask him to decide on the specific items that need further work and to note these in the space provided. *This may require some guidance from the teacher.*

Evaluation
The pupil is able to target areas that require further practice. The teacher is in a position to decide on the most appropriate teaching strategies to use.

Self Evaluation Checklist

Name .... Class .... Date **R7**

I sit correctly.	YES [ ]	NO [ ]
My tool hold is correct.	YES [ ]	NO [ ]
My non writing hand is placed on the paper correctly.	YES [ ]	NO [ ]
I need to use a tool grip.	YES [ ]	NO [ ]

1. My letters are formed correctly.	ALL [ ]	MOST [ ]	SOME [ ]	NONE [ ]
2. My tall letters are the correct height.	ALL [ ]	MOST [ ]	SOME [ ]	NONE [ ]
3. My letters with tails are the correct length.	ALL [ ]	MOST [ ]	SOME [ ]	NONE [ ]
4. My middle size letters are the same size.	ALL [ ]	MOST [ ]	SOME [ ]	NONE [ ]
5. My oval letters are closed.	ALL [ ]	MOST [ ]	SOME [ ]	NONE [ ]
6. The straight lines of my letters are straight.	ALL [ ]	MOST [ ]	SOME [ ]	NONE [ ]
7. The slant of my letters is regular (parallel).	ALL [ ]	MOST [ ]	SOME [ ]	NONE [ ]
8. My letters sit on the lines correctly.	ALL [ ]	MOST [ ]	SOME [ ]	NONE [ ]
9. The spacing between my letters is even.	YES [ ]			NO [ ]
10. The spacing between my words is even.	YES [ ]			NO [ ]
11. My capital letters are formed correctly.	ALL [ ]	MOST [ ]	SOME [ ]	NONE [ ]
12. I use capital letters correctly.	YES [ ]			NO [ ]
13. I use full stops correctly.	YES [ ]			NO [ ]
14. I join my letters.	ALL [ ]	MOST [ ]	SOME [ ]	NONE [ ]
15. My horizontal joins are correct.	ALL [ ]	MOST [ ]	SOME [ ]	NONE [ ]
16. My diagonal joins are correct.	ALL [ ]	MOST [ ]	SOME [ ]	NONE [ ]
17. My numbers are formed correctly.	ALL [ ]	MOST [ ]	SOME [ ]	NONE [ ]

I need to work on:

1. ....

2. ....

3. ....

© Jane Taylor, *Handwriting: A Teacher's Guide*, David Fulton Publishers, 2001

Teaching Strategies using the 'Rules'

This section of the manual offers some alternative teaching strategies for older pupils that can equally well be used with younger pupils.

Handwriting is 'rule' based (Alston and Taylor 2000), and if the rules are applied to handwriting then legibility can be achieved. Offering the pupil a rule changes the emphasis from the teacher dictating what should be done to a situation where the pupil is in control. Rules are a useful *aide-mémoire* that, if applied and practised, should make a dramatic improvement to a pupil's handwriting.

Remember to praise the pupil for what he has already achieved before offering any teaching strategies. Before embarking on the working with the rules, time should be taken to introduce **The Four Ps** (p. 50). It may be necessary to work on **Joins** (p. 67) before introducing a rule. Do not introduce more than one rule at a time. The following instructions should be used for each rule.

> **Instructions**
> 1. Decide on the letter that needs to be corrected.
> 2. Check whether other letters within the 'family' are correctly written. If there is a correctly written letter compare the similarities and differences.
> 3. Give the rule to the pupil and ask him to repeat the rule.
> 4. Demonstrate the letter on the white board. Indicate the movement pattern with arrows. Ask the pupil to look carefully at the direction of the arrows.
> 5. Cover the letter and ask the pupil to write the letter on the white board.
> 6. If the letter is correctly formed ask him to write it out three times.
> 7. Ask him to decide which are the well-formed letters and to give each one a tick. This gives the pupil the opportunity to become self-critical and the teacher the opportunity to be constructively critical.
> 8. Ask him to repeat the rule.
> 9. Ask him to close his eyes and to write out the letter again. *A successful attempt indicates that the pupil has begun to internalise the letter form. This task may be repeated two or three times. If the pupil is still having difficulty move on to another letter in the same family and come back to the previous letter in the next session.*
> 10. Ask the pupil to write the letter in his exercise book. If it is correctly formed ask him to write out the letter three times.
> 11. Ask him to decide which are the well-formed letters and to tick each one.
> 12. Ask him to write out the letter repeatedly for a given number of seconds. The amount of time chosen will depend on the pupil's ability. *This task may be repeated two or three times.*
> 13. Ask him to write two words that start with the letter just practised.
> 14. Ask him to tick the letter just practised if it is well formed.
> 15. Ask him to write out one sentence using at least one of the chosen words.
> 16. Ask him to tick the letter just practised if it is well formed.
>
> **Alphabet Speed (A13)** (p.64) can be used for further practice or to monitor progress.

Rule 1: Letters that end on the base line have an exit stroke

This rule applies to a pupil who is using print script. He will need to learn to write the letters which end on the base line with an exit stroke before he can begin to learn a cursive script.

Rule 2: All letters except **d** and **e** begin at the top of the letter

This is a useful rule for a pupil who does not start letters at the correct place.

Or: All letters start on the base line

This rule applies to pupils who are learning to begin every letter with an entry stroke.

Rule 3: Oval letters should be closed

Letters **a d g** are often written with a gap at the top because the oval letter is started at the 12 o'clock position instead of at approximately 1 o'clock.

Rule 4: All similar letters are the same height

Many pupils do not appreciate that letters come in three heights and this can be established by asking the pupil to place plastic letters on a single line (see **Appreciating the relative height of letters**, p. 57). Once the pupil has used the plastic letter and appreciates the relative heights of letters the teacher can select a letter that caused difficulty and follow the instructions at the beginning of this section. The pupil might find using three-line paper helpful. Alternatively, he may prefer to use the **E4** guide lines placed under his sheet of paper so as to be faintly visible.

Rule 5: All letters relate to the base line

Letters relate to a base line whether it is visible or not. The body of a letter and exit strokes should sit on the base line.

Rule 6: Straight lines should be straight and parallel

Irregular slant is a common problem. Straight lines are found in 18 letters: **a b d f g h i j k l m n p q r t u y**. A regular slant is achieved when the straight lines are parallel.

The pupil may find it helpul to use the **E5** guide lines (p. 9). The line guide can be placed under the sheet of paper on which the pupil is working so as to be faintly visible.

Rule7: Spacing between letters should be even

Regular spacing is much easier to achieve when the pupil has learned to use exit strokes on letters. Check that the pupil is using exit strokes appropriately before introducing this rule. First explain and demonstrate how spacing can be improved by paying attention to exit strokes and joins. It may be necessary to work on incorrect joins at the same time as improving spacing (see **Joins**, p. 67).

Rule 8: Spacing between words

The spaces between words should be equal.

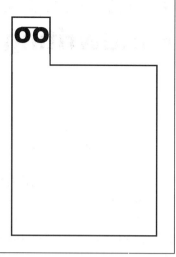

Figure 12 Word spacer

Equipment
Take a small piece of card. Cut out the 'spacer' (see Figure 12). In the left-hand corner ask the pupil to write the letter **o** twice. For the left-handed pupil reverse the card and place the **oo** in the right-hand corner.

Instructions
1. Ask the pupil to write a sentence.
2. Ask the pupil to place the 'spacer' between each word and to give the space a tick if it is approximately the same size.
3. Give the pupil the rule.
4. Explain to the pupil that, in order to maintain an equal space between words, it is necessary to look back at the space already left between previous words.
5. Ask the pupil to write out another sentence.
6. Ask the pupil to use the 'spacer' to check whether his spaces are equal and to tick those that are.
7. Repeat this exercise two or three times.

Rule 9: A sentence begins with a capital letter and ends with a full stop

The concept of using a capital letter at the beginning of a sentence and a full stop at the end is difficult to grasp. Some pupils may find this rule helpful. It is important that the full stop is placed in the correct position (see **Punctuation**, p. 66).

Joins
Some pupils may be using print script; others may be forming joins incorrectly. A pupil who is using print script will need to spend time practising putting exit strokes on to letters which end on the base line before he learns how to join letters (see **Joins**, p. 67).

Numeral formation
Incorrectly or poorly formed numerals will need to addressed (see **Learning to Write Lower and Upper Case Letters and Numerals – Task 7**, p. 60).

Teaching typing
A number of pupils, despite their attempts to improve their handwriting, will never achieve fluent, legible handwriting. They will need to use a word processor for all written work. Once it has been decided that a pupil should use a word processor, it is imperative that he first learns to touch type; he will also need to master IT skills. There is no quick and easy way to learn to type, but by working conscientiously and with application the skill can be mastered. There is no perfect software program so using more than one offers variety (see **Typewriting/keyboard programs**, p. 83).

Identifying Underlying Causes of Poor Handwriting

The expectation of the NLS is that most pupils will have achieved automatic, legible, fluent, speedy and attractive handwriting by the end of Year 4 (DfEE 1998). However there are likely to be one or two pupils in every class who find the acquisition of efficient handwriting difficult. This may imply that they have underlying cognitive, psychosocial, sensorimotor, visual perceptual, coordination, language, dyslexic, attention deficit and/or hyperactivity difficulties. It is important that a pupil's difficulties are brought to the attention of the special needs coordinator as a matter of urgency so that the dysfunction can be investigated. In some cases it may be necessary to refer the pupil on to an appropriate professional person (e.g. an educational psychologist or speech and language therapist). Most frequently, referrals are to a paediatric occupational therapist or a paediatric physiotherapist, whose programmes aim to remediate 'the child's underlying dysfunctions in different performance components' (Chu 1997). However, there is often a long waiting list both for assessment and for subsequent treatment. During this waiting period there is a great deal that the teacher can do. If she does not have suitable assessment procedures and a handwriting programme, the manual can be used for guidance to establish these. Furthermore, many of the pupils would benefit from a structured physical education programme.

Our understanding of brain function is still in its infancy. Henderson *et al.* (1998) suggest that the development of classification schemes of motor disorders seems to have proceeded without any real empirical justification and that there is very little data pertaining either to the elements within the classification schemes or to the broader issues that need to be addressed. There tends to be an overlap of the elements within each group.

Whitmore *et al.* (1999) suggest that the term 'dysfunction instead of disorder acknowledges poor (impaired) performance, which, from observation can be categorically specified, without implying a known specific defect'.

At present the most commonly categorised dysfunctions are dyslexia, Attention Deficit Disorder (ADD), Attention Deficit Hyperactivity Disorder (ADHD), Developmental Coordination Disorder (DCD) and dyspraxia.

Dyslexia

Dyslexia can be described as

> a combination of abilities and difficulties which affect the learning process in one or more of the following: reading, spelling, writing and sometimes numeracy/language. Accompanying weakness may be identified in the speed of processing, short-term memory, sequencing, auditory and/or visual perception, spoken language and motor skills. Some children have outstanding

creative skills, others have strong oral skills, whilst others have no outstanding talents, they all have strengths. Dyslexia occurs despite normal intellectual ability and conventional teaching; it is independent of socioeconomic or language background. It is however, more easily detected in those with average or above average intelligence.

(British Dyslexia Association (BDA) 2000)

Attention Deficit Disorder (ADD) and Attention Deficit Hyperactivity Disorder (ADHD)

A child can be predominantly inattentive, unable to concentrate on any job, activity or lesson. Others display extreme hyperactivity or there may be a combination of both types. The cause may be physiological or emotional or both. Typical symptoms are: inattention, poor concentration, impulsiveness, hyperactivity/over activity, disorganisation, poor social skills, insensitivity to others, aggression and contentiousness. A structured environment and short attainable goals suit these children best (Hawley 2000).

Developmental Coordination Disorder (DCD)

DCD is diagnosed in children 'who experience movement difficulties out of proportion with their general development and in the absence of any know medical condition (e.g. cerebral palsy) or identifiable neurological disease' (American Psychiatric Association (APA) 1994). In the past these children were given the label 'clumsy'. The World Health Organisation's *International Classification of Diseases 10* (ICD10) (1992) uses the term 'Specific developmental disorder of motor function' (SDDMF) and this is the term that is being adopted by the National Health Service in Britain.

Dyspraxia

Dyspraxia is an impairment or immaturity of the organisation of movement. Associated with this there may be problems of language, perception and thought. It includes what to do and how to do it (Dyspraxia Trust – now the Dyspraxia Foundation – information leaflet). Dyspraxia is also referred to as sensory-intergrated dysfunction.

Useful checklist and tests

The list below is not intended to be comprehensive.

- The **Movement Assessment Battery for Children** (Henderson and Sugden 1992a,b) provides a means of identifying and evaluating gross and fine movement problems.

  Included in this battery of tests is a checklist that teachers can use to screen 'at risk' pupils. The manual provides guidelines for management and remediation and will assist the teacher to plan suitable PE intervention programmes.

- The **Developmental Test of Visual-Motor Integration** (Beery 1997), age range 3–18 years, measures a pupil's eye–hand coordination. This is a shape-copying test which begins with a vertical line with the shapes gradually becoming more complex. In addition there are two supplementary tests that measure visual perception and motor coordination.
- The **Test of Visual-Motor Skills TVMS-R** (Gardener 1995), age range 3–13 years 11 months, measures a pupil's eye–hand coordination and tests motor accuracy, motor control and motor coordination.
- The **Test of Visual-Perceptual Skills (non-motor) TVPS-R** (Gardener 1996), age range 4–12 years 11 months, measures visual discrimination, visual memory, visual spatial relationships, visual form constancy, visual sequential memory, visual figure ground and visual closure. There is an upper level for 12–18-year-olds. In addition the Test of Auditory Perceptual Skills (TAP) measures areas of auditory perception. The value of this test is that it is non-motor.

Useful programmes

Many pupils who have poor handwriting find manipulating scissors difficult.
- *Developing Scissor Skills* (Mahoney *et al.* 1997) provides an excellent short programme that will assist the pupil to learn this skill. Specialist scissors that assists a pupil in learning how to hold scissors correctly are available from PETA UK.

Pupils with DCD benefit from additional PE input so that their gross motor abilities can be improved in tandem with the learning handwriting skills.

- **Hands up for Handwriting** (Handwriting Interest Group (HIG)) is a 'workout' session preparing the hands for handwriting.
- *Movement Assessment Battery for Children Manual* (Henderson 1992b), Chapters 9–14, focus on the cognitive-motor approach to intervention.
- *Take Time* (Nash-Wortham and Hunt 1997) focuses on various aspects of movement with suggested activities.
- **Write from the Start**, previously sold as the *Teodorescu Perceptuo-Motor Programme* (Teodorescu and Addy 1997) is a useful programme for the pupil aged 4–7 with marked perceptual difficulties. It has over 400 carefully graded exercises and activities to develop hand–eye coordination, form constancy, spatial organisation, orientation and laterality.

Typewriting/keyboard programs

- **Keyboard Pro** available from iANSYST, The White House, 72 Fen Road, Cambridge CB4 1UN.
- **Typing Instructor DeLuxe** available from iANSYST, The White House, 72 Fen Road, Cambridge CB4 1UN.
- **Micro-Type**, a program specifically developed for pupils with dyslexia, available from IEC Software, 77 Orton Lane, Wombourne, South Staffs WV5 9AP.

Glossary

Automatic Without conscious effort.

Cognitive Intellectual ability.

Cursive script A running hand.

Engram The physical trace of a memory in the brain.

Ergonomics The scientific study of the relationship between workers, their environment and machinery.

Exit strokes The linking together of letters by one or more strokes.

Fine motor skills Fine body movements concerned with the wrist, thumb and fingers.

Gross motor skills Large body movements concerned with trunk, arms and legs.

Kinaesthetic feedback The brain's sense of the body's positioning, the perception of muscle movement.

Legibility Ability to be read easily.

Ligature The linking together of letters by one or more strokes.

Lower case letters Small letters.

Motor A muscle for moving part of the body – a nerve exciting muscular action

Motor dysfunction Movement impairment of a muscle for moving part of the body – a nerve exciting muscular action.

Perception The mental action of knowing external things through the medium of sense presentations.

Perceptual dysfunction Impairment of the mental action of knowing external things through the medium of sense presentations.

Phonology The sounds and combination of sounds in a particular language.

Praxis The ability to plan, organise and execute purposeful skilled movements.

Print script Letters are written without exit strokes.

Psychosocial Emotional state and behaviour.

Sensorimotor The innate mechanism that enables the individual to be aware of the body.

Upper case letters Capital letters.

Visual perception The interpretation and the use of what is seen includes – mechanics of vision, visual attention, visual discrimination, spatial relationships, form constancy, visual closure, visual figure ground, visual memory.

Visual-motor The ability for the hand to interpret what the eyes perceives.

Resources

Equipment

- *Adapted pens.* (Aremco)
- *Dycem.* A non-slip material which can be placed under a workbook to prevent it from moving. (Nottingham Rehab)
- *Pencil grips, Tri-Go and Grippies (e.g. Stubby grip).* (LDA Living and Learning)
- *Plastic letters (without exit strokes).* (Taskmaster)
- *Posture Pack (writing slope and wedge).* (Children's Seating Centre)
- *Roll 'n' Write Alphabet (with exit strokes).* (LDA Living and Learning and Philip & Tacey)
- *Roll 'n' Write Numbers.* (LDA Living and Learning and Philip & Tacey)
- *Special scissors.* (Peta UK)
- *Tactile Sandpaper Letters Cursive Style.* (Philip & Tacey)
- *Tactile Sandpaper Numbers.* (Philip & Tacey)
- *Tri-Go grip.* (LDA Living and Learning and Taskmaster)
- *White Plastic A4 Board, with writing lines at the bottom on one side and squares on the reverse.* (Philip & Tacey)
- *Wooden Diagraphs and Trigraphs (cursive script).* (LDA Living and Learning)
- *Wooden Letters Capital and Lower Case (with ligatures).* (Taskmaster)
- *Wordbuilding Box (wooden letters with ligatures).* (LDA Living and Learning)
- *Write Angle.* (Philip & Tacey)

Suppliers (equipment and publications)

- Armeco, Grove House, Lenham, Kent ME17 2PX (Tel: 01622 858502).
- Children's Seating Centre, 11 Whitcomb Street, London WC2H 7HA (Tel: 020 7930 9308).
- Dextral Books, 43 Norwood Avenue, Didsbury, Manchester M20 5EX (Tel: 01061 4450159).
- LDA Living and Learning, Wisbech, Cambs PE13 2AE (Tel: 01945 463441).
- Nottingham Rehab, Ludlow Hill, West Bridgford, Nottingham NG2 6HD (Tel: 0115 9452345).
- Peta UK, Mark's Hall, Margaret Roding, Dunmow, Essex CM6 1QT (Tel: 01245 231811) www.peta-uk.com (accessed December 2000).
- Philip & Tacey, North Way, Andover, Hants SP10 5BA (Tel: 01264 332171).
- QED, The Rom Building, Eastern Avenue, Lichfield, Staffs WS13 6RN.
- Taskmaster, Leicester LE2 6BR (Tel: 0116 270 4286).

Other useful resources

- **Anything Left Handed**
  5 Charles Street, Worcester WR1 2AQ (Tel: 01905 25798)
  www.scoot.co.uk/anything_left_handed (accessed December 2000)
  Specialist in products for left-handeders. They supply an excellent video: *Left-Handed Children – Guide for Teachers & Parents*.

- **Handwriting for Windows**
  KBER, 50 Kennedy Road, Shrewsbury, Shropshire SY3 7AA (Tel: 01743 356764)
  A programme which allows the teacher to produce handwriting worksheets and other documents in simulated handwriting.

- **Specific Learning Difficulties Resources Booklet**
  Gillian Hawley, The King's Mill House, Great Shelford, Cambridge CB2 5EN (Tel: 01223 843125)
  This A4 booklet is full of useful information, although some of the information is orientated to the East Anglia region.

- **Write Dance**
  Ragnnhild Oussore Voors, Lucky Duck Publishing, 23 Wellington Part, Bristol BS8 2UW (Tel: 0117 9732881) www.luckyduck.co.uk
  A progressive music and movement programme for the development of pre-writing and writing skills.

Useful Addresses

Handwriting Interest Group (HIG)

The HIG, formed in 1983, is a multidisciplinary forum that aims to promote an active interest in the acquisition of handwriting skills by organising study days and publishing a journal, *Handwriting Today*, formerly the *Handwriting Review*, and relevant booklets.

Contact the Membership Secretary at 5 River Meadow, Hemingford Abbot, Huntingdon PE18 9AY.
www.handwritinginterestgroup.org.uk (accessed December 2000).

HIG publications, available from Ann Markee, Blackthorn Farm, Snows Lane, Keyham, Leicester LE7 9JS, are:

- *Handwriting – Are You Concerned? A Basic Guide for Parents*
- *Tools of the Trade*
- *Hands up for Handwriting*

National Organisations for Dyslexia, Dyspraxia and Attention Deficit/ Hyperactivity Disorder

British Dyslexia Association (BDA)
98 London Road, Reading, Berks RG1 5AU (Tel: 0118 966 2677)
www.bda-dyslexia.org.uk (accessed December 2000)

Dyslexia Institute
113 Gresham Road, Staines TW18 2AJ (Tel: 01784 463851)
www.dyslexia-inst.org.uk (accessed December 2000)

The Hornsby International Dyslexia Centre
Wye Street, London SW11 2HB (Tel: 0207 223 1144)
www.hornsby.co.uk (accessed December 2000)

The Helen Arkell Dyslexia Centre
Frensham, Farnham, Surrey GU10 3BW (Tel: 01252 792400)
www.arkellcentre.org.uk (accessed December 2000)

Dyspraxia Foundation
West Alley, Hitchin, Herts SG5 1EG (Tel: 01462 455016)
www.emmbrook.demon.co.uk/dyspraxia (accessed December 2000)

ADD Information Services
PO Box 340, Edgware, Middx HA8 9HL (Tel: 020 8905 2013)
www.addiss.co.uk (accessed December 2000)

Bibliography

Addy, L. (1997) 'On the write lines', *Special Children* Autumn, 65–7.

Alston, J. (1990) 'Aspects of handwriting in primary school children'. Unpublished PhD thesis, University of Manchester.

Alston, J. (1992) 'Assessing writing speeds', *Handwriting Review*, 102–6.

Alston, J. (1994) 'Written output and writing speeds', *Dyslexia Review* 6(2), 6–12.

Alston, J. (1995) *Assessing and Promoting Writing Skills*. Stafford: NASEN.

Alston, J. and Taylor, J. (1987) *Handwriting: Theory, Research and Practice*. London: Croom Helm.

Alston, J. and Taylor, J. (1988) *The Handwriting File*. Wisbech: LDA Living and Learning.

Alston, J. and Taylor, J. (2000) *Teaching Handwriting: A Guide for Teachers and Parents*. Lichfield: QED.

American Psychiatric Association (APA) (1994) *The Diagnostic and Statistical Manual of Mental Disorders 1V*, (DSM 1V). Washington, DC: APA.

British Dyslexia Association (BDA) (2000) *The Dyslexia Handbook*, I. Smythe (ed.). Reading: BDA.

Berninger, V. and Graham, S. (1998) 'Language by hand: a synthesis of a decade of research on handwriting', *Handwriting Review*, 11–25.

Brown, B. and Henderson, S. E. (1989) 'A sloping desk? Should the wheel turn full circle? *Handwriting Review*, 55–99.

Beery, K. E. (1997) *Developmental Test of Visual-Motor Integration*. Cleveland, OH: Modern Curriculum Press.

Chu, S. (1997) 'Occupational therapy for children with handwriting difficulties: a framework for evaluation and treatment', *British Journal of Occupational Therapy* 60(12), 514–20.

Chu, S. (2000) 'The effects of visual perception dysfunction on the development and performance of handwriting skills', *Handwriting Today* 2, 42–55.

Department for Education and Employment (DfEE) (1998) *The National Literacy Strategy – Framework for Teaching YR to Y6*. London: DfEE. (www.standards.dfe.gov.uk/literacy/publications/?pub_id=135&top_id=327&atcl_id=2100, accessed December 2000).

Department of Education and Science (DES) (1989) *English in the National Curriculum*. London: HMSO.

Diekema, S. M. *et al.* (1998) 'Test-retest reliability of the evaluation tool of children's handwriting manuscript', *American Journal of Occupational Therapy* 52(4), 248–55.

Dutton, K. (1989–90) 'Writng under examination conditions: establishing a baseline'. Scottish Education Department/Regional Psychological Services, Professional Development Initiatives, New Demands and Responses. (Also in *Handwriting Review* 1992, 80–95.)

Gardener, F. M. (1995) *Test of Visual-Motor Skills TVMS-R*. Hydesville, CA: Psychological and Educational Publications.

Gardener, F. M. (1996) *Test of Visual-Perceptual Skills (non-motor) TVPS -R*. Hydesville, CA: Psychological and Educational Publications.

Handwriting Interest Group (HIG) (1999) *Tools of the Trade*. HIG Publications (available from Ann Markee, Blackthorn Farm, Snows Lane, Keyham, Leicester LE7 9JS).

Hasbrouck, J. *et al.* (1994) 'Objective procedures for scoring student's writing', *Teaching Exceptional Children* Winter, 18–22.

Hawley, G. (2000) *Specific Learning Difficulties Resources Booklet*. Cambridge: Gillian Hawley.

Hedderly, R. G. (1995a) 'The assessment of SpLd pupils for examination arrangements', *Dyslexia Review* 7(2), 12–16.

Hedderly, R. G. (1995b) 'Sentence completion test', *Dyslexia Review* **7**(2), 19–21.

Henderson, S. and Barnett, A. L. (1998) 'The classification of specific motor coordination disorders in children: some problems to be solved', *Human Movement Science* **17**(4–5), 435–47.

Henderson, S. E. and Sugden, D. (1992a) *Movement Assessment Battery for Children (Movement ABC) Checklist.* Sidcup: The Psychological Corporation.

Henderson, S. E. and Sugden, D. (1992b) *Movement Assessment Battery for Children Manual.* Sidcup: The Psychological Corporation.

Mahoney, S. *et al.* (1997) *Developing Scissors Skills: A Guide for Parents and Teachers.* Dunmos: Peta (UK) Ltd.

Mandal, A. C. (1985) *The Seated Man.* Klampenborg, Denmark: Dafnia Publications.

Michael, B. (undated) *Purposeful Drawing.* Glasgow: Jordanhill College of Education.

Nash-Wortham, M. and Hunt, J. (1997) *Take Time*, 4th edn. Stourbridge: The Robinswood Press.

New Zealand Department of Education (1979) *A Study of Handwriting of Form 1 Pupils in New Zealand Intermediate Schools.* Wellington: New Zealand Department of Education.

Oussore Voors, R. (1995) *Write Dance.* Bristol: Lucky Duck.

Pickard, P. and Alston, J. (1985) *Helping Secondary School Pupils.* Wisbech: Learning Development Aids.

Qualifications and Curriculum Authority (QCA) (2000) *Curriculum Guidance for the Foundation Stage.* London: QCA. (www.qca.org.uk/ca/foundation/guidance/curr_guidance.asp accessed December 2000)

Ramsden, M. (1992) *Putting Pen to Paper.* Crediton: Southgate Publisher.

Russell, J. (1988) *Graded Activities for Children with Motor Difficulties.* Cambridge: Cambridge University Press.

Sassoon, R. (1983) *The Practical Guide to Children's Handwriting.* London: Thames and Hudson.

Sheriden, M. D. (1975) *From Birth to Five Years: Children's Developmental Progress.* Windsor: NFER-Nelson.

Taylor, J. (1995) 'The sequence and structure of handwriting competence: where are the breakdown points in the mastery of handwriting?', *British Journal of Occupational Therapy* July, 205–7.

Teodorescu, I. and Addy, L. M. (1997) *Write from the Start.* Wisbech: LDA Living and Learning.

Thomas, F. (1997) Workshop presentation, HIG INSET course, Institute of Education, London, November.

Thomas, F. (1998) 'Une question de writing: a comparitive study', *Support for Learning* **13**(1), 43–6.

Thomas, S. (1997) 'Near-point gripping in pencil hold as a possible disabling factor in children with SEN', *British Journal of Special Education* **24**(3), 129–32.

Thomson, M. E. and Watkins, B. (1990) *Dyslexia: A Teaching Handbook.* London: Whurr Publishers.

Wallen, M. *et al.* (1996) *The Handwriting Speed Test.* Adelaide: Helios.

Whitmore K. *et al.* (1999) *A Neurodevelopmental Approach to Specific Learning Disorders.* London: Mac Keith Press.

World Health Organisation (WHO) (1992) *International Classification of Diseases 10* (ICD10). Geneva: WHO.

Ziviani, J. (1984) 'Some elaborations on handwriting speed in 7–14-year-olds', *Perceptual and Motor Skills* **58**, 535–9.

Ziviani, J. and Watson-Will, A. (1998) 'Writing speed and legibility of 7–14-year-old school students using modern cursive script', *Australian Occupational Therapy* **45**, 59–64.

Other useful publications

Alston, J. (1990) *Writing Left Handed.* Manchester: Dextral Books.

Alston, J. (2000) *Teaching Spelling: A Guide for Teachers and Parents* (previously published as *Spelling Helpline*). Lichfield: QED.

Alston, J. and Taylor, J. (2000) *Teaching Handwriting: A Guide for Teachers and Parents* (previously published as *Handwriting Helpline*). Lichfield: QED. (A useful booklet that elaborates the rules of handwriting.)

Hornsby, B. (2000) *A Walk-through Guide to Alpha and Omega.* London: The Hornsby International Dyslexia Centre. (A workbook designed to teach the alphabet in capital letters. Pictures are provided to increase phonological awareness.)